GUIDE TO A WELL-BEHAVED PARROT

PARROT

Mattie Sue Athan

With Photographs by Susan Green,
Mattie Sue Athan, and Lisa Lalone
Drawings by Michele Earle Bridges

Consulting Editor: Matthew M. Vriends, Ph.D.

BARRON'S

To my family.

Photo Credits
Sara Frances: page 15;
Bucy: page 95.

About the Author:

Mattie Sue Athan is one of a handful of bird behavior consultants in private practice in the United States. Since the mid 1970s, she has studied the development and modification of behavior in parrots living as companions with humans. While much of her early work dealt with wild-caught birds, since the 1980s the bulk of her practice has been with domestically-raised parrots. She is particularly interested in the development of behavior problems such as aggression, screaming, and self-mutilation in hand-fed birds. Her work has appeared in *Bird Talk Magazine, American Cage Bird Magazine*, *The Pet Bird Report*, *Positively Pets*, and numerous other specialty publications.

All inquiries should be addressed to:
Barron's Educational Series, Inc.
250 Wireless Boulevard
Hauppauge, New York 11788

International Standard Book No. 0-8120-4996-9

Library of Congress Catalog Card No. 92-38559

Library of Congress Cataloging-in-Publication Data

Athan, Mattie Sue.
   Guide to a well-behaved parrot / Mattie Sue
Athan ; drawings by Michele Earle-Bridges ;
consulting editor, Matthew M. Vriends.
      p.   cm.
   Includes bibliographical references
and index.
   ISBN 0-8120-4996-9
   1. Parrots—Behavior.   2. Parrots—Training.
I. Vriends, Matthew M., 1937–   .   II. Title.
SF473.P3A84   1993
636.6'865—dc20   92-38559
                                                        CIP

PRINTED IN HONG KONG
20 19 18 17 16 15 14 13

Important Note:

Parrots may develop aggressive and unpredictable behavior as they grow older. Even usually-sweet, formerly hand-fed, domestically-raised parrots, particularly large mature birds, can do permanent, irreparable damage to human faces and hands. When handling mature parrots of any size, human control should be carefully maintained at all times. Eye protection is recommended, particularly when handling unfamiliar mature parrots.

Companion parrots, even apparently healthy ones, may be carriers of salmonella, ornithosis, and tuberculosis, all of which may be infectious to humans and other companion animals. The presence of parrots in the home should be mentioned during any medical consultation for human illness or allergies.

Contents

Foreword

Mattie Sue Athan and I started working with parrots about the same time. This was back in the "dark ages" when parrots were just starting to gain popularity as pets in this country. People tried to rely on their intuition to figure out why their pets acted the way they did. Unfortunately, this is often still true. Many owners, who have great expectations of a wonderful relationship with their pet parrot, become completely frustrated as their birds begin to have serious behavioral problems. It seems that no matter what the people try, their parrots still bite, scream, pluck their feathers, hate the owner's spouse, reject any foods but seed, become phobic, refuse to come out of the cage or won't be tamed. Some owners listen to everyone and try everything. They try to resolve their parrot's behavioral problems with advice intended for breeding birds, dogs, cats, or human children. Their lack of understanding about "parrot psychology" often makes the problems worse.

Fortunately, need usually creates a response. A few people throughout the country who have a great love and special understanding about pet parrots started working to help the frustrated bird owner with their problems. Although Mattie Sue and I started with the same dedication in the mid 1970s, we have just recently become acquainted. Although we often tell different stories and use different words to describe our ideas and techniques, we definitely have the same philosophies. We both feel that taming is based on patiently winning a parrot's trust. We both respect the intelligence of parrots and feel that they need guidance and rules to be good pets. We both believe that parrots are highly reactive to their owner's behavior and that a parrot can't change unless the owner changes. We both share an intense love for the curious comical nature of parrots.

As the editor of the *Pet Bird Report*, a publication featuring behavioral information, I am often asked by parrot owners if there is a good book that deals with pet parrot behavior. So much of the information available is either outdated or deals with parrots as breeders rather than human companions. I am delighted that I can now answer, "Yes, there is a good book that deals with parrot behavior!" and refer them to Mattie Sue Athan's *Guide To A Well-Behaved Parrot*.

Sally Blanchard

Preface

Lakewood Seed and Pet was the most incredible store I had ever seen. An anachronism even in the 1970s, it looked like a country feed store with a couple of dozen parrots on open perches, numerous free-roaming kittens, and water lilies in wading pools in the front window.

One day, as I bent over the cat toys, I felt someone lift the little billfold from my hip pocket. Turning swiftly, I confronted an enormous blue-crowned Amazon, eyes flashing, gaily chewing on my wallet. I retrieved the wallet, but my heart was stolen away.

The blue crown, called Esmiralda, was sold, so I put money down on a baby yellow nape due to arrive soon.

Six months later, after bringing in a small sum every Saturday afternoon, the bird was mine!

A few weeks after Portia came home, I received a call from the owner of what would become one of the most famous pet stores in the West, Colorado Seed and Pet. Gale Whittington said that since I had stopped coming in on Saturdays, the other birds in the store weren't as nice. Would I consider a business arrangement that included "hanging out" in his store on Saturday afternoons?

So I was drafted. Within a short time I was driving many miles every Sunday to help other people "socialize" their parrots in their homes. It

appeared that I could do things with the birds that they wouldn't tolerate from anybody else, and that their behavior was changed after interacting with me.

At that time, most of the parrots in my little corner of the world were caught in the wild; little was known about the extent to which their behavior could be modified. Many of them required initial socialization that was then called "taming." I was horrified that so many of the books available in pet stores recommended harassing the bird with gloved hands and a straight, hand-held perch, when it seemed so much better to touch and massage them gently. Many of those same books are still on the market advising "stick training"—a practice I find mostly counterproductive.

Of course, I soaked up every bit of parrot behavior information within my means. In the beginning, when most of my work involved taming, I studied the work of cat behavior consultants. By the mid 1980s, I was seeing more captive-raised, hand-fed birds. As my work with captive-raised parrots increased, I studied dog behavior consultants. And I soon came to understand that I also had to study human behavior.

Much of what I did was still bird training. But I learned that if I simply showed people how to handle their birds to achieve a desired response, my clients frequently were unable to sustain the pattern. If I did not spend time training *the people*, the re-sponses were not reinforced, and the session was ultimately unsuccessful. I had to learn how to tell people things they didn't want to hear in ways that would enable them to listen. Psycho-therapist Jill Owen trained me to say the same thing in several different nonjudgmental ways.

Many times I went into a home to find that my clients had all the right information and instincts, but they simply didn't know how to apply them. Sometimes the people didn't have a clue how to relate to the bird, but were highly motivated to do so. I also learned that the birds' behaviors were favorably modified with the techniques I used and that those techniques could be learned by almost anyone who tried to learn them.

Denver was, and still is, a small, isolated city. When I ask who recommended me to a particular client, they still sometimes reply, "Everyone." Every parrot owner I met asked where to find a book on companion parrot behavior. This book, 14 years in process, was written to answer the questions I heard over pizza in hundreds of homes.

I would like to thank everyone who has ever asked me to help with their parrot behavior problems and my family and business associates who tolerated much neglect while I pursued the happy hookbill. I must also thank Dr. Matthew Vriends, Sally Blanchard, Mary Kaye Buchtel, Chloe St. Clair, and a host of others who were always available to chew on an idea.

Chapter 1

Who, What, When, and Where?

Parrot "Behaviorism"

Whether it is alone or in the company of others, a happy bird is a playful bird.

How many people have grown up with an ornery parrot? Remembered as a vicious creature with a nasty disposition, it terrified strangers and children with equal ferocity. Nobody played with it; nobody, (except, possibly, its owner) touched it. Nobody dared. Nobody cared. At best, it was fed regularly, but usually it was no more than an amusing ornament.

Life isn't much different for many pet parrots today, but change is on the horizon. We are increasingly aware that this highly intelligent creature is capable of exceptionally interactive behavior—almost surpassing pet status to become a friend and companion. Indeed, humans are forming remarkable relationships with feathered alter egos who talk to us in our own voices, scream to welcome the delight of morning, and snuggle up for affection in the night.

Training is the key to this radical lifestyle change in the companion parrot. No one would consider living with an untrained Doberman. No one would think of returning an untrained puppy because its behavior wasn't perfect. We now know that training, particularly aggression-prevention training, is just as relevant for companion parrots as for companion dogs.

Companion parrot "behaviorism" is a new and exciting body of knowl-

edge growing daily from the works of a handful of individuals who are sharing remarkably similar, independently obtained information. This book provides basic tools for training and behavior modification in parrots to ensure the successful companion relationship between parrots and humans. Behavior modification for parrots usually involves observation of the bird and its environment, the taking of a history, physical examination, and evaluation of the bird's responses to handling. Most common treatments include environmental and dietary manipulations, improved discipline and handling skills, and planned modifications of responses to stimuli.

The parrot is an aggressive, territorial creature who wishes to have total control of the immediate environment. Like rottweilers and some teenagers, without tough, loving discipline, an untrained parrot frequently matures into a truculent, angry martinet who uses raw force and a temperamental nature to manipulate its surroundings. A baby parrot ignored during the developmental period will teach itself behaviors such as biting or screaming rather than learning all the wonderful ways to enjoy living with humans. An untrained companion parrot faces a very restricted life at best.

With proper training, I believe a parrot can be a loving companion throughout its lifetime. With parrots, as with dogs, behavior modification is best begun early. Since many large

hookbills have a lifespan similar to humans, "early" lasts longer for parrots than for their short-lived canine friends. Since they are more intelligent than dogs, most emotionally healthy parrots can be trained at any time of life, except when they are experiencing seasonal hormonal activity and the related insanity that accompanies these periods. Any training initiated later in a parrot's life must progress more slowly.

Sensitivity and appropriate reactions are usually essential to modifying parrot behavior, but young birds are so adaptable that they may even do well without them. Consider the following anecdote:

I was once called to evaluate a young cockatoo. From the telephone interview, it sounded as if the unfortunate owners had a vicious creature on their hands, but I am reluctant to give advice over the telephone because I know I must see the bird and the environment.

The bird was a previously unhandled imported young adult, probably two to six years old — an age at which it should be easily trainable. The white cockatoos are among the few Psittaciforms that show some slight gender difference (sexual dimorphism). This bird had the reddish brown eyes of a (behaviorally desirable) female, but the caller said she had an "attitude" and he was considering getting rid of her. I couldn't schedule an appointment for several days, so I advised the owner to switch to passive interaction (see page 17) rather than actual physical contact until I arrived.

When I walked into the house, it was immediately apparent to me that the bird was crazy about her new family. From across the room, she mimicked their approximate syllables, gave them coy looks, and exhibited several characteristic happiness behaviors.

When I tried to handle her, she lacerated my hands. It was obvious that she was not right physically. I discovered that she had a dislocated hip, a very painful injury. This wild bird was befriended, almost taught to step up onto an offered hand by a novice who didn't realize that her leg had been pulled from the hip joint. The bird loved him anyway. She just didn't want to be touched because she was in pain!

A veterinarian had diagnosed a "bruised leg" which would "be alright with time." When the owner realized the situation, he took the cockatoo immediately to an avian veterinarian who x-rayed the leg and referred them to a university facility for hip surgery on this very sweet bird.

Parrot behaviorism is not training parrots to do tricks. Only a few rudimentary behaviors, like stepping onto an offered hand, are necessary for good social interaction, I believe parrots should be encouraged, within certain limits, to be themselves. While I have nothing against trick training — better for a bird to learn socially acceptable tricks than to improvise unacceptable behaviors — my objective is the necessary happy adjustment between parrots and the humans who live with them. Most frequently I am asked to modify aggression and clear up miscommunications between birds and owners. That involves asking the owners and the parrot what is wrong, then explaining to each of them how to meet the other's needs.

Sometimes, the bird literally tells me the problem. In one case the owners suspected that their 17-year old Eleanora cockatoo — a large bird — was ready to breed. He was biting unpredictably, and all efforts to modify the behavior had failed. The evaluation revealed a very self-confident bird who was bloodying all humans without provocation. For years he had been a "teddy bear" who loved handling; now he tolerated no touch. If you even stood too close, you needed Band-Aids. Sitting in their kitchen that sunny morning, I asked the bird what was the problem.

He looked me straight in the eye and said, "I'm gonna get married."

His owners of 17 years, a retired couple, nearly fell off their chairs. They assured me that he had never been taught to say that, and they couldn't imagine where he had ever even heard that expression. His attitude and words were very clear to me; they immediately began advertising for a mate.

A companion bird may overtly dislike another pet or human. About a third of my work involves love triangles in which a bird bonds strongly to one member of a couple and tries to drive the other half out of the house. It can be a real ego blow when the pet your spouse or lover bought for *you*, which was the most expensive gift *you* ever got, falls in love with *your significant other* and tries to hurt you. Human/avian "love triangles" are particularly disconcerting when the bird periodically changes loyalties.

For the most part, I see each client only once or twice a year. Usually, a few hours spent with a human/avian family tells them all they need to know to understand each other, and I become obsolete. Like a therapist, I probably haven't done my job if someone doesn't weep with joy, relief, or painful insight during the process. Following are easily accessible solutions to a majority of the behavior problems I see in companion parrots.

This Is the Parrot

A parrot is not a dog or cat. A gregarious parrot will demand *more* attention than a dog; a reclusive one will expect *less* attention than a cat. Because there are many different types of parrots and because of extreme differences in their genetic makeup, up-

Parts of the Parrot

1. Cere
2. Forehead
3. Eye ring
4. Iris
5. Ear coverts
6. Back of head
7. Nape of neck
8. Bend of wing
9. Mantle
10. Back
11. Median wing coverts
12. Greater wing coverts
13. Secondaries
14. Primaries
15. Tail
16. Foot
17. Abdomen
18. Breast
19. Lower mandible
20. Upper mandible

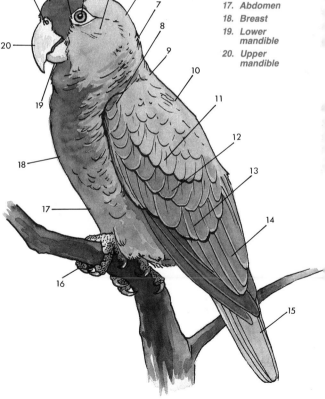

bringing, and socialization, there is great variation in behavior between types of parrots as well as between one individual parrot and another of the same type.

A bird's primary defense mechanism is escape. It is a throwback to a time when safety could be reached by merely flying away. That time may have passed. Some people believe that birds are the direct descendants of dinosaurs and are on the brink of sharing their fate. Certainly the parrot resembles the dinosaur more than it resembles the dog or cat. Birds are disappearing at an alarming rate; many of them exist, like dinosaurs, only in historic memory. We live with fewer than a third of the species of birds that were alive 200 years ago.

A parrot is a bird with a notched upper mandible (beak); a mallet-shaped tongue; and four toes, two opposing two. A healthy parrot sleeps on only one foot. Larger parrots, like raptors, are vulnerable to few natural predators, and unlike all birds except raptors, parrots have taste buds. They can see in more than one direction at a time.

The parrot is an omnivore, a creature who eats food from both vegetable and animal sources. Today's understanding of the dietary needs of parrots has been based largely on research done in the poultry industry. Because there are so many different types of parrots from so many varied habitats, it is reasonable to assume that the dietary requirements of one parrot may vary somewhat from the

needs of a similar parrot; and that any parrot's needs probably vary greatly from the dietary requirements of a dissimilar parrot from another part of the world. We know without question that female parrots require more calcium and related nutrients necessary to assimilate calcium when they are laying eggs. It is probably safe to assume that the greater the variety of fresh, nutritious foods a companion parrot consumes, the more likely the bird will achieve its nutritional requirements.

Parrots Act Like People

Like humans, some parrots blush (obvious in macaws because of their bare face patch), use tools, remember past incidents, and communicate with language. For the most part, parrots are monogamous and not sexually dimorphic. That is, most species have no observable differences between the genders. With few exceptions, they are long-lived creatures for whom the successful rearing of young is difficult. Because they are cavity breeders, carving chambered nests usually out of tree trunks or limbs,

their actual nesting behaviors have probably been more closely observed in captivity than in the wild. A pair of mature parrots may take several years of trying before they successfully rear offspring. Several of the larger species raise no more than one or two babies a year; sometimes they raise one or two babies every other year. It is a process over which they exercise choice. They may choose to abandon or destroy the nest, eggs, and/or babies at any time they perceive the area or food supply to be insecure.

A large, green-naped scarlet macaw baby.

One tidbit of parrot lore tossed around from time to time says, "The parrot has the intelligence of a three-year-old human with the emotional development of a two-year-old human." I don't know who said it, but it's not far off the mark, and that's a pretty volatile combination. It means that a companion parrot may be more able to manipulate the behavioral environment than a toddler and will have extremely selfish motives in doing so. It means that violent jealousy is often present. It means that intellectual and environmental stimulation must be provided to prevent the development of long-term behavior problems.

Thy People Shall Be My People

As individuals, parrots are very adaptable. Wild-born parrots captured relatively young (under two years) often adjust superbly to the captive environment, even to the extent of establishing themselves as the dominant member of the social group within a few years. Wild-caught individuals occasionally surpass home-bred hand-feds as companions to humans. Parrot-type birds can usually be tamed more quickly, easily, and successfully at a later age than feral domestic cats.

A parrot will usually flee from perceived danger but aggressively do battle with a sibling or flock member over the slightest element of control over the home environment. A mature parrot may aggressively defend its personal territory against even the most enormous and fearsome intruder. One of the most charming Christmas parrot stories tells of a macaw's successfully rebuffing a burglar who intruded into "his" pet store. They say the police, responding to a late night call, discovered an angry macaw marching up and down the pet store aisles and *cursing*. They captured the injured burglar nearby.

In addition to vast intellectual differences between same or like-species birds, early socialization plays a pivotal role in the social, behavioral, and emotional development of a parrot. There are in companion situations with humans still parrots that were captured from the wild. They usually differ significantly from the hand-fed offspring of domesticated parrots. Some of the factors which influence these differences are:

Bonding

Although it does not exactly imprint like some other baby birds, the young parrot attaches itself psychologically to the perceived parent. Depending upon whether the baby bird was fed by birds or with human hands, it might relate to human hands as "mom" or "the enemy."

How the juvenile bird learns and adapts to its place in the human/avian social group influences the bird's long-term behavioral and emotional adjustment.

Behavioral History

The parrot develops behavioral patterns in response to past experiences of being captured, mistreated, under nurtured, or over nurtured.

The parrot loves routine and will frequently develop behavioral "rituals." For example, one companion bird might insist on a kiss or a head scratch before stepping up onto an offered hand; another bird might always cough whenever it sees a cigarette smoker sitting on the sofa.

When falling asleep, a well-adjusted parrot grinds its lower beak against the inside of the upper mandible, making a sound not unlike persons grinding their teeth in their sleep. This activity is grooming for tomorrow's eating, and a sick or depressed bird may neglect this important part of personal hygiene. A malnourished, sick, or depressed parrot may have shape deformities of the lower mandible from omission of beak grinding.

A relationship with a parrot has the potential to be *extremely long*. Both humans and birds will go through many life changes. The stages of the human/parrot relationship are more like human parenting stages than the canine or feline life cycle. The baby bird will be a baby almost as long as a human baby and will learn to communicate fundamental needs in much the same way. The toddler will require firm, loving supervision, with both rules and opportunities for successful decision making. The teenager will be an emotional roller coaster. There may be a long period of emotional parting when the bird is allowed to mate. There will be bereavement at your passing—for if provided with a healthy lifestyle, a large hookbill acquired as a baby by an adult human will probably survive that person.

For a successful companion relationship to last and the mutual admiration society to be maintained, it is reasonable to expect the parrot's behavior to be socially acceptable to humans. Of course, the bird's learning socially acceptable behavior depends on the owner's willingness to set a good example and provide good training.

It was not the fault of Pol, Andrew Jackson's yellow-headed Amazon parrot that she was removed from her owner's funeral for "crude language." Like dogs or cats with behavior problems, companion parrots with behavior problems such as foul language, screaming, feather chew-

Well-socialized companion birds are always ready to interact with friendly, confident humans.

ing, or aggression are at risk of having an unhappy future. If they have monetary value and are successful breeders, they might get lucky and wind up with someone with husbandry expertise. Because of their relatively low monetary value, loud calls, temperamental and high-strung natures, conures are at particular risk of both overt abuse and neglect.

Both partners in this emotionally symbiotic relationship—humans and parrots—have a right to a happy life together. It is the responsibility of the humans to provide for the physical and emotional needs of the bird. Indeed, clear-cut human expectations contribute greatly to the parrot's happiness, for one of the bird's strongest drives involves understanding and securing an *exact* place in the pecking order.

Chapter 2
Early Interactions

Passive Games Birds Like to Play

Some parrots communicate by imitating human speech. More frequently they learn to understand limited verbal communication from their humans. The most dependable channel of communication with a parrot, however, is body language—nonverbal cues one individual gives another.

An astute owner learns to read a parrot's mood by the position of the bird's feathers. Depending upon the way they are held, ruffled head feathers may be an invitation to pet, an aggressive warning, or a sign of illness.

The companion parrot also learns to read human body language. A well-adjusted pet may be drawn to almost any personality type, but a wary new bird will more easily trust steady, placid people who don't move their heads or hands when they talk. Active children or animated conversationalists who punctuate words with gestures confuse and frighten shy birds.

Successful communication with a new bird should not include objects or behaviors that create the feeling of being hunted or captured. Avoid gloves and sticks. Approach with games and passive interaction to gain the trust of a wary parrot.

The following games include both verbal and nonverbal passive interactions. Different parrots will favor different games. Individual pets will learn to play the games in different sequences, but all types of parrots in all stages of tameness enjoy playful, passive interaction. Humans, however, must identify and learn the games birds like to play.

Stage 1, Games for Shy Birds

I couldn't possibly look at you: Eye contact is threatening to a shy parrot, so one must mimic the bird's behavior. Look away if you catch the bird looking at you. Turn your head, cast your eyes down, or otherwise hide your eyes (*not* with hands) until the bird is comfortable looking at you and letting you look back.

I can be shorter than you: With a puppy, you play fighting/domination games like "I am bigger and tougher than you!" One may also play roughhouse games with some domestic

Playful parrots can turn any interaction, no matter how innocuous, into a game.

hand-fed parrots, but most new birds (particularly wild-caught ones) prefer to play more passive games. Because a creature on a level lower than the bird is less threatening, situate yourself so your eyes are always lower than the bird's eyes.

I can be a statue: A variation of "I can be shorter." If the parrot freezes when looked at, try holding still longer than the bird. (Moluccan cockatoos love this game!)

I am more frightened than you: You come around the corner quickly; the bird is startled, screams, and flops off the perch. Counter this reaction with body language that indicates you are more terrified than the bird (but don't scream). Make yourself very short, hide, or calm yourself by slowly rocking back and forth and by

Even a normally interactive parrot might turn its back to a person it doesn't like.

making cooing sounds. This will show that you are frightened while also calming the panicked bird.

I don't have hands: Since you are trying to impress this feathered, fingerless creature with your similarities, prevent the bird from seeing your hands. Approach a parrot in the most non-threatening manner with your "wings" folded (hands in pockets or behind back).

Stage 2, Games for Birds That Are Somewhat Steady

Blink back: An animal experiencing fear will not blink while maintaining eye contact with an assumed aggressor. Initiate communication by seeking eye contact then closing your eyes. An interested, interactive parrot will close its eyes or "blink back" with a new friend if it, too, is growing trustful. If the bird is very fearful, it will not blink while you are maintaining eye contact.

Peep-eye (peek-a-boo): A curious parrot growing accustomed to new surroundings will wonder where people go when out of sight. It will stretch to see around corners or climb around for a better view. A human friend might also peer around corners and reading materials for a look at the parrot's private activities. Try combining this game with "Blink" and "I can be shorter..."

I can sleep in front of you: A bird looking down on a sleeping human is not afraid. Sometimes while sneaking a peek from a reclining position, you may first observe a new bird preening, tail wagging, "shaking out" or exhibiting other happiness behaviors.

I like to touch and be touched: If you ultimately wish to caress your parrot, demonstrate the joy you feel when touching a loved one or another pet. Showing your appreciation of loved ones and pets will also help your bird feel comfortable in their presence. Be cautious, because in the future this game might stimulate jealousy and overt or displaced aggression. Be sensitive to the responses you are observing.

Tap, tap, tap: Many parrots will tap a foot or beak, apparently to intimidate, when staring down a human. A respectful but unfrightened human sitting across the room might tap back the same rhythm with a pencil, fork, or finger. This game is the audio version of "Blink" and may be initiated by a curious, more confident bird.

Stage 3, Games for More Confident Parrots

Let's get rowdy together: Many birds will vocalize loudly along with a favorite song, an appliance, or a broadcast sports event. Bird buddies are usually eager to vocalize with noises in their environment, whether it's a living room or a jungle. Create a social bond by joining your bird in a good scream.

I'm calling yooouuuooouu!: A curious parrot will want to know where you are, even if it cannot see you. The bird will call out, and if you answer, it will call back. This is a favorite parrot-initiated game and an excellent way to teach a bird to speak for attention. It's also a great way to teach a parrot to scream, so watch that volume.

Rituals: All birds in a flock seek food, eat, shower, groom, scream, and perform other necessary physical functions in unison. Your parrot will demonstrate its connection with you by eating when you eat, bathing when it hears running water, grooming, laughing, and screaming at the dog when you do these things. Encourage your bird to develop nonviolent, nonsexual rituals.

Stage 4, Games for Well-Socialized Companion Birds

Anything you can do, I can do, too: Once a bird feels comfortable, it will stretch, shake out, or wiggle its tongue with no reservations. A bird delights in humans who mimic these behaviors. Like a kitten, a healthy parrot will greet human friends with a long, slow stretch. Owners who observe a bird stretching a greeting by extending a wing and a leg might "parrot" the parrot's behavior. This would demonstrate a similar feeling of well-being and happiness in the company of a friend.

I can give you food, and you will eat it: Many birds will take food from a hand, then drop or throw it. Try mimicking the bird's behavior. Drop or throw the food once or twice, wait a few minutes, then offer the food again. A happy, well-adjusted bird will accept food and eat it. If the bird will not take food from your hand *and eat it*, go back to Stage 1 or 2.

I'll drop it, and you pick it up: Quite possibly, this is the game most frequently initiated by parrots with humans. Almost every parrot owner can relate a story or two about this most frustrating game. Some people will play it, and some people are just too proud. I believe any human who will spend a few moments picking up a repeatedly dropped trinket for a bird is well on the way to being a trusted, treasured friend for life.

I will wear toys for you: All tame birds know that eyeglasses, jewelry, buttons, and shoelaces are worn solely for *their* entertainment. Carry hold-and-chew toys to substitute for unapproved chewables when socializing with your bird. For safety's sake, select pierced earrings with backs that pop off easily, and don't expect to have easy-to-thread shoelaces. Those little plastic tips resemble new feather sheaths and will be promptly removed if accessible.

Tug-o-war: It's not okay to let the bird win *all the time*, particularly if it is an aggressive bird; but be sure to let a shy bird win often.

Rescue me!: Also a favorite parrot-initiated game with several frightening variations. **Help, my toe is caught!** is a version well loved and frequently played by Amazons. It was certainly the favorite game of Portia, my yellow nape, during his bachelor days. (Yes—this Portia proved to be a male!) He would flap, scream, and hang upside down by a single toe. When his concerned owner rushed to help, she found a delighted bird (not stuck) gleefully displaying for attention. This game is exciting, though a little hard on the heart. A loving owner must check the bird in case it really is in trouble!

Chase me!: This is a slightly controversial game because it isn't passive, and one must be sure that *the bird* wants to play. (Never chase a frightened parrot if you have a choice.) The concept of this game is that there is running and chasing, *but no catching*.

Chase Me! is a favorite game of Goffin's cockatoos and is sometimes mistaken for fearful or untame behavior. I am often called to tame a "bronco" Goffin's whose owners were convinced that the bird didn't like them. "She comes to me, but when I try to touch her, she takes off like a shot," confused humans would say.

Usually, I found a doting bird that ran from even the most mundane contacts—not in fear, but for fun. Some Goffin's will literally run circles around the person they want to chase them. If you want to handle these little beauties, entice them with passive body language, wait and reward them—with petting, not food—for coming to you.

A parrot's games will vary with the passing of time from shy baby games to more sophisticated challenges and flirtations. These interactions will remain a delightful part of your lives together. Playful passive interactions are a great way to relate to a tame parrot that needs attention when everyone is too busy to handle it.

Passive noncontact games are absolutely the best way to interact with a bird that doesn't like being touched. Simply because the parrot won't tolerate the hand doesn't mean it isn't a playful pet. Certainly, the more creativity and imagination you devote to a pet's games, the more enjoyable will be your time together.

Aggression Prevention: Training for Successful Long-term Relationships

Whether the "new" parrot is a hand-fed baby or a wild-caught bird, training should begin as soon as the bird is comfortable, but not yet territorial, in the home. Just as dogs learn to understand commands given in "people talk," parrots trained with consistent techniques learn to respond consistently to verbal and physical stimuli. A well-defined authority-based relationship and well-reinforced interactive behaviors will overlay tendencies for aggression that develop when the parrot reaches sexual maturity.

In dog training the down/stay command not only provides the dog with a socially acceptable behavior; it reinforces the respectful loving relationship with primary humans. The response to the command is dependent upon the authority-based relation-

Care must be taken to ensure that birds are merely tearing up their toys, not swallowing the pieces.

ship's consistent reinforcement. The dog may respond perfectly to one family member and avoid responding to another. The failure to respond may be due to the manner in which a command is delivered or by "failure" in the authority-based relationship.

With a parrot, the primary behavior usually considered necessary for successful interactions with humans is stepping up onto the offered hand without biting. But reinforcing the step-up command does more than merely teach an appropriate behavior; it establishes the power hierarchy between humans and bird.

The parrot's natural tendency is to want to dominate. I once had a treasured videotape of the 20/20 television program on animal intelligence. Dr. Irene Pepperberg is featured with her African gray parrot Alex, who gives the good doctor a number of commands: "Come here"; "I want banana"; "Go pick up corn." I showed this tape to demonstrate that if a bird talks with cognition, probably what it most likes to do is *give orders*.

The parrot is a naturally assertive, domineering, and demanding creature that will, upon maturity, have hormonally induced "temper tantrums." Training, preferably early training, is essential to avert the development of aggression. It is desirable that the bird's primary humans handle it with the same techniques. To achieve a consistent response, each person must prompt for the step-up command in the same way and hold the bird in the same way.

I believe that allowing the bird to perch on the forearm takes away human control. In addition, because the skin of the forearm sometimes "rolls" (especially in women) and is difficult for the bird to grip, this practice can sometimes cause the unsteady bird to bite. With the exception of budgies and most cockatiels, it is also a mistake to allow a parrot to perch on the shoulder at will. This is of particular significance in the presence of others (humans or birds) of whom the bird might be jealous.

The appropriate place for a parrot is on the hand. A "hand-trained" bird will go willingly to the hand. A poorly trained bird will constantly try to run up the forearm or jump to the shoulder. The following simple handling tips combined with subsequent reinforcement should easily remedy this situation.

The "Egyptian" Grip

Because the bird's primary instinct is to climb *up*, training the bird to stay on the hand can easily be accomplished if hand and arm are always held in the same way—with the hand as the highest point the bird can attain without climbing down. The Egyptian grip is designed to take advantage of this climbing instinct. Sitting at a desk or table, place your elbow on the surface in front of you with fingertips held together pointed toward the ceiling. With the thumb folded into the palm, bend the wrist so that the index finger is approximately parallel to the floor, tips slightly angled upward. The fingers are held straight, rigid and together, with the thumb folded into the palm. Avoid raising the base of the thumb or the elbow as the bird attempts to go "up" the arm (which is no longer *up* if the elbow is *down* and the forearm is *perpendicular to the floor*).

Go to the Corner

Teaching the bird to step from hand to hand can be accomplished in a hall with all the doors closed or in a blocked-off corner with no external visual or auditory stimulation and no possibility of escape. Sit on a carpeted floor so that if the bird falls or tries to flee, it won't have far to fall and the landing will be as soft as possible. As soon as the bird figures out that there are no alternatives to cooperation, cooperation will quickly be achieved. This process works best if the bird *thinks* it has some choice in the matter and if it *thinks* it is being enticed rather than being forced.

Begin step up training with good grooming. If the bird has full wings, there will often be dispositional problems as well as the temptation to fly. If the bird has sharp nails and a sharp beak, the handler may wince and give unintentional anxiety signals to the bird.

When first learning to step up, some birds may be frightened and unsure. Approach initially with soothing words and petting. If the day and the bird are hot, keep a fine-mist spray bottle of water handy to keep the bird cooled down. If the bird is nippy, it may be best initially to cover

The "Egyptian" grip is designed to take advantage of the bird's climbing instinct.

the hand with a solid color towel, then gradually remove the towel so that the bird is standing on the hand. Work with the bird a couple of times a day for 15 to 25 minutes, sensitively observing the bird's responses.

Accidental Messages

When handling the bird, pay special attention to controlling the messages you are giving the bird with your body. Use the words "Good bird" before a desired behavior such as "Step up" to stimulate the bird to respond positively to the prompt. Always quit on an "up note" or when a successful response has been achieved. If the bird is put away following a negative incident such as a bite, that behavior has just been unwittingly reinforced. Verbal praise and laughter are particularly strong reinforcement tools. It is important never to laugh when your favorite feathered comrade bites another person.

Some people have trouble responding verbally without moving their head. Because the bird will understand body language better than human speech at this time, head movements may give the bird confusing, contradictory, and unintended messages. A shy bird will react negatively to head nodding; an interactive, human-bonded bird might respond positively; an over-stimulated, hormonal bird might attack someone who punctuates speech with head movement.

Height Factors

During this initial training period, hold a shy bird so that its eyes are higher than the eyes of the human teaching the step-up response. If the bird is aggressive, work it at chest height, with eyes below chin level. If everyone who handles the bird consistently uses exactly the same handling mannerisms and reinforces a successful response, the bird's confidence will grow. As the bird becomes more and more self-confident (this may be from the very beginning with a baby parrot) the relative height of the eyes is lowered so that the bird must look up into the eyes of the handler. In the case of many hand-fed babies, the bird must be held lower than the mouth of the handler to prevent later development of aggression.

As the bird steps from hand to hand, there may be a temptation to bite. There will probably, at least initially, be the tendency to test the stability of the offered perch (the hand) with the beak. If the bird places the beak upon the hand and the hand is snatched away, both insecurity and the bite will be further reinforced. It is important to allow the bird to put its beak upon the offered hand to build trust with the handler. I believe this may be the bird's logic during this phase: "If I have my beak on a person, I can injure. If I am not injured, I won't inflict injury!" Allowing the bird to put its "hand" (beak) on the "perch" (human hand) builds the trust and confidence of bird and handler alike.

The Wobble Correction

There may be a time early or later during the training of step-up when the bird will bite the offered hand. At this point it is almost always a mistake to shake the bitten or nearly bitten finger in the bird's face. This is an invitation to fight, even if the shaken hand or finger is in a superior position. Even if this form of correction is momentarily effective, the bird's ire will resurface at some point. If the bird is sitting on the hand or a hand-held perch, an appropriate and effective response is to wobble (or shake, if the bite is vicious) the *hand the bird is sitting on*. When the bird loses balance, it will discontinue the bite. If the bird learns that a bite usually brings a wobble, it will discontinue the behavior.

Be aware that a wobbly hand or perch *can cause* a bite. The initial prompt to step up must be firm, steady, and trustworthy or the bird might bite rather than step up. The bird must be firmly placed on the hand or it might fall rather than be corrected by a wobble.

Don't Hit

I do not advocate hitting the bird at anytime. If you hit too hard, you might injure the bird. (I once worked with a very remorseful human with a large arm bandage and macaw with a black eye!) It is not difficult to further enrage the bird and perpetuate the cycle of violence.

Don't Grab the Bird's Beak

Early in my career, I was advised to train a biting bird not to bite by restraining its upper mandible in the hand. I now believe that this practice is dangerous. It is not unlike grabbing a person's hands and nose. It is an insulting and infuriating act. It can also damage the bird.

This does not mean that very sensitive, playful beak locking is always inappropriate. Birds frequently lock beaks with one another, but grabbing an angry bird's beak will further enrage the poor bird.

Don't Reinforce Biting

Many seemingly logical responses to biting can reinforce the behavior. The very best way to respond to a bite or attempted bite from a young bird is to ignore it. If appropriate behaviors are consistently reinforced, any behavior that is not reinforced will quickly disappear.

Reach an Understanding

These techniques (1) let the bird know what is expected so that it won't have to guess or improvise behaviors with each handler and (2) reinforce the authority-based relationship with humans.

The step-up command should be so ingrained in the bird that no hesitation is involved in performing the response. A well-trained parrot will lift its foot if it wants to be picked up or if someone says "Step up" from across the room. This is boot camp for the battlefield. Someday the bird will be experiencing raging hormone attacks. The bird's aggressiveness can then be sidetracked with a decisive glare and a well-timed "Step-up!" command.

The Way to a Parrot's Heart: Befriending the Steady but Reluctant Parrot

When socializing an unhandleable parrot, at some point domination techniques must give way to "befriending." The following information will take a bird who has learned through domination to "step up" past the point of merely tolerating human handling so that it can become an adoring creature who seeks its owner's company. Building a loving relationship with a bird is easily accomplished with the use of gifts or rewards.

With cockatoos, cockatiels, and full-sized macaws, petting is often the "gift" of choice. With eager mimics like parakeets, African grays, and some Amazons, singing and verbal praise are eagerly sought rewards. Many birds enjoy a mutual head bob or mimicking stretch.

But what do we do with a willful little parrot who has figured out how to be unfriendly and doesn't like petting and doesn't seem to care whether we talk or not?

Fine spray-mist baths work for some birds sometimes, but edible treats from the hand remain the time-tested rewards of choice. Feeding from the hand not only ensures a balanced avian diet; it can build a warm and trusting relationship between humans and the birds who share their homes. Feeding mimics nature, as courting parrots feed each other to enhance their bond as well as survive the nesting period.

A little observation will determine what the new bird's favorites are. Many macaws favor spaghetti, and several species love apples, grapes, or corn on the cob. Recent imports almost always go for sunflower seeds.

A bird may favor Cheerios or popcorn. The bird's *very favorite food in the whole world (VFF)* never reaches the food bowl. Instead, the food bowl contains the other 90 percent or so of a perfectly balanced diet. The bird consumes that portion of the diet at will.

Begin by offering the treat from below the bird: that is, the bird is higher than the human and the treat. At first the bird may drop the hand-given treat or throw it. The trainer might establish communication by mimicking the bird's behavior, then reoffering the treat until it is accepted. The treat might first be placed near the bird, on the cage or perch. The bird might not eat it until the trainer sits down, moves away, or leaves the room.

Except for some high-strung species like the Goffin's cockatoo, a well-handled, normally adjusted bird will learn to take its VFF from a human hand and eat it within a few days. A bird learning to take food from the hand usually should not be required to learn anything by domination techniques—including, "step-up" and "petting practice" —but merely be repeatedly enticed to eat its VFF. If the bird stops eating and taking food after "step-up" and "petting practice," then this process is going too fast or is not being accomplished sensitively, and handling techniques should be reevaluated.

A bird that has been in a home for more than three months that will not take its VFF from a human hand and eat it may need professional help.

Eventually, the bird seeks out the

human treatgiver, as most parrots fall hopelessly in love with the hand that holds the corn on the cob (or grapes or sunflower seeds).

How to Pet a Parrot: Enticing the Hand-shy Bird to Seek Petting

When the hand is presented, a tame parrot will step up on it. A "teddy bear bird" will fluff its neck feathers and tuck its head under or against the hand for petting. What a joy it is when your bird nuzzles its head under your finger for the first time!

When introducing a parrot to the joys of petting, the bird's enjoyment of the process is the most important factor, so obvious domination techniques usually don't work well; in fact, they might do more harm than good. Some force is involved, but it is gentle, subtle—more like a dance or mutual seduction. The bird is introduced to a gradually increasing level of pleasure that overcomes its natural aversion to physical contact with humans.

Practice: Teaching a reluctant bird to enjoy touching requires a practiced, accomplished bird petter versed in avian pleasure techniques. These are acquired skills that can be learned by petting birds that already enjoy human touch. Tame Moluccan and umbrella cockatoos are commonly "teddy bear" birds and willing participants in petting practice.

Usually, most parrots do not naturally enjoy petting in the direction feathers grow. Not only does it offer little sensation, but the feeling it affords replicates their "wary" expression (the holding of feathers smoothly against the body).

Most hookbills prefer petting gently across or against the direction of feather growth. To understand how this feels, run your hand along the surface of your hair in the direction of growth. Then insert fingers under your hair and gently caress both across the direction of growth and against the direction of growth. Which is more pleasing?

It is not important to touch the skin. Since feather shafts are rigid, it is necessary only to move feathers in the appropriate direction to induce pleasure; this can be done with the breath. Even if a bird likes a little skin contact, move from place to place to avoid irritation.

Blood feathers or pin feathers (the ones that still have a blood supply)

Parrot petting is a skill that can be learned. Start by practicing on birds that obviously enjoy petting.

must be petted gently with or across the feathers. This means that a bird that normally enjoys petting against the feathers may prefer with-the-feather petting during molting. This phenomenon is not to be underestimated. Some birds really like to be petted with the feathers, although many merely tolerate it because it's the only way they get petted at all. The sensitivity of the petter to evaluate the bird's response is most important here. Mary Kaye Buchtel reports that eclectus parrots, in particular, prefer with-the-feather petting.

Most birds react negatively to touching of wing and tail feathers. Also avoid the breast to avoid confusion with the step-up prompt. Almost any other place on the body might be considered an erogenous zone by a typical parrot. Pay special attention to ears, nostrils, eye rings, beak, under the beak, wing pit, the bony ridges along top underside of wings, under the tail, on top of the tail (oil gland) and the neck. Many cockatoos enjoy being gently stroked on the bald spot under their crest. Most birds who enjoy petting like a little squeeze from a hand cupped under the wings and over the back. Be careful with this one, though, because many birds find this sexually stimulating and may develop aggressive tendencies.

The jaw is a particular favorite of most parrots. Wiggle a finger along the lower edge of the jawbone; approaching the lower mandible, the bird may turn its head upside down to accommodate the finger. Larger parrots may appreciate a little probing into the cavity under the lower beak where the tongue rests when the beak is closed. Some cooperative birds will yawn when petted in a circular motion at the intersection of upper and lower jawbones.

Spend time gently pulling the feathers. Grasp them near the base or about midway and roll or slide fingers toward the tip. This is particularly effective in the presence of blood feathers, as a solitary pet bird usually has no bird buddy to "unwrap" incoming new feathers. The casing on a mature blood feather should be broken off no closer than 1/3 inch (.8 cm) from the blood supply. This approximates a bird behavior called alopreening.

Observe: A parrot experiencing pleasure will fluff up the feathers on the area being caressed. It may close its eyes or make appreciative noises. Although the bird will be very still, it

A parrot asking to be petted might lift a foot and scratch its own head, neck, or jaw.

may alter its position to accommodate petting in desired areas. When successful hand contact is discontinued, there will be happiness behaviors—puffing feathers, shaking out body or wings, and tail wagging. A completely mesmerized bird will remain motionless when petting is discontinued.

A parrot inviting petting may strike a glazed, come-hither look, puff up its neck feathers and lower the head. An untame parrot may exhibit postures inviting contact, then react badly when you try to touch it.

Restrain and pet: Since many parrots are prejudiced against gloves (because of handling during import or in the pet trade) and towels (because of improper or insensitive veterinary exams or grooming), begin petting training by restraining a reluctant parrot in a down vest or jacket. Almost any garment will do, although it may wind up with a hole or two.

Cradle the bird gently in the restraint garment and pet it with hands hidden from sight. It is probably unnecessary to actually restrain the bird in the garment, as most soon realize they really enjoy petting. Never restrict the in-and-out movement of the bird's chest.

Speak softly and constantly, slipping a bare hand up to pet under or over the base of the tail. Try to pet the bird's cheek, nostrils, or jaw without it seeing fingers.

Observation and sensitivity are the keys to success in this project. Because this technique works for some birds and not others, be sensitive to the bird's behavior and prepare to modify the approach if the bird's response is negative.

Don't push too hard, but don't back off too soon and reinforce resistance on the part of the bird. A bird may *act distressed* during handling, but it may not really *be distressed*. Watch for the absence or presence of happiness behaviors such as preening or tail wagging when hand contact is removed.

Again, it is not necessary to actually pet a bird on the skin, but merely to move the feathers, which may be done with a warm, gentle breath directed to the neck.

A bird that will allow foot stroking may then permit petting up the thighs, under or over the tail, along the back to the neck, being careful not to touch the wings. I believe many "touch freak" birds first learn to hold their wings up for wing-pit petting because their first instinct is raise them to avoid having their wings touched during petting.

Pet, then *back off and observe*. If the bird expresses happiness response (shake out and/or tail wag) within two minutes, continue. If the bird looks uncomfortable and/or tries to get away, then try a different approach or go more slowly. This learn-to-be-petted process must not be interpreted by the bird as domination, but rather enticement.

Some birds respond to being petted on the oil gland on top of the tail at the base of the spine. Insert fingers

Many birds enjoy being petted on the back under the wing. Care must be taken, however, that this is not perceived sexually by the bird.

under and into the feathers for maximum pleasure and also to hide them from the bird's sight. From the area of the oil gland, proceed under wings or up the backbone to the neck and head.

On a training stand: Some hand-shy birds tolerate petting with a pencil or other small inanimate object. A bird on a chest-level training stand may be distracted with one hand and touched with the other. If the bird bites at one hand, approach with the other. Touch the bird briefly in a place where petting is usually enjoyed by other similar types of birds, then gradually increase contact time.

Reward: Accompany each handling session with generous rewards of loving words, showers, or treats.

Some trainers withhold favorite food items — grapes, sunflower seeds, peanuts, or peppers — from the bird's normal diet except from the hand. This deprivation training or operant conditioning works very well if you can figure out what the bird wants.

Reaction: A bird may temporarily discontinue taking favorite foods immediately after training sessions. Demonstrative birds may snatch the treat, then drop or throw it. Try mimicking their behavior, that is, drop or throw the treat, wait a few minutes, then offer the treat again. This phase should pass within a few days or something is wrong.

Again, this process is more like a courtship, with the human teacher displaying shy and sensitive body language while becoming progressively more bold.

Watch for signs of regression—less passive interaction, excessive biting, or refusing favorite treats on a regular basis. Back off if the bird is not showing improved tolerance and/or enjoyment of petting. Give more rewards, go more slowly, and start over. Don't pressure the bird or repeatedly force it to do something it doesn't want to do.

Modeling: A hand-shy bird might be induced to allow petting if it observes another bird enjoying petting. If no other bird is available, try petting another person. Have a human "second student" compete for attention when you are trying to pet the bird; then notice the second student, spend time petting and softly speaking to the second student, and watch the bird's reaction.

Don't underestimate the value of soft lights and sweet music. No matter how wild the parrot, woo gently, and the cuddles will come.

Establishing Social Dominance: Twelve Steps to an Effective Authority-based Relationship

Once the companion parrot is feeling comfortable and established in its home territory, it may begin a very obvious struggle to "rule the roost." It is important at this time to set ground

---

The Head Squeeze

Many birds enjoy what essentially amounts to a cranial massage. This "head squeeze" can be accomplished like this: while engaging in neck and head petting, slide the thumb over one ear, index and middle finger back over the head, knuckle of ring finger over the other ear and gently squeeze. Feel the shape of the skull and jaw. Some birds will become totally mesmerized by this special massage technique.

---

rules for a healthy, effective, authority-based relationship in which the bird is well aware that humans are the boss—not the reverse.

Reward: Reward and reinforcement are essential to the effective authority-based relationship. Warm, friendly praise is all many parrots need. An untame parrot may be rewarded with food or bath treats, but most tame birds probably respond best to praise or petting. Verbal praise in anticipation of a desired behavior will often stimulate the bird to perform the behavior that is being prompted.

Give permission: Give permission if the bird is about to do the action anyway. (This does not include jumping onto the shoulder at home!) For example, say "okay" when Paco is starting to chew on an approved chewable; "okay" when your bird

starts to eat dinner. This is a comfortable setup that's easy to establish so that the bird learns to look to you before improvising what may be unacceptable behavior.

Deny permission: Monitor the bird's behavior; teach manners. Even if the bird is allowed treats from the table, don't let it jump on the table and walk through the plates. The bird should have its own place and dishes for eating with the human "flock," and it should be required to wait its turn, not just jump on Mom/Dad and grab the spaghetti off the fork.

Step-ups: A very simple way to reinforce the authority structure. The step-up response should be so automatic that the bird will lift a foot if you say "step up" from across the room. It should even discontinue a fierce hor-

monal rage if you make strong eye contact and give the command.

Establish a dependency relationship: The bird should know it must cooperate for something it wants. For example, you might require your bird to do a few simple exercises before you give dinner, a favorite toy, or time at liberty. If the bird learns to associate the activities, it will learn to cooperate, lest it not receive the anticipated rewards. Parrot behavior consultant Sally Blanchard suggests requiring the bird to step up on the hand in order to leave the cage. This dependency upon the human hand as the only way out of the cage should inspire a bird to be very cooperative.

Don't let a "demon lover" sit on your shoulder: In a parrot's home territory or in the presence of a rival, this is an unquestionable error. When a parrot is experiencing seasonally aggressive behavior, allowing the bird on the shoulder is an invitation to facial stitches; you could wind up with a broken nose, a crooked smile, or you could lose an eye.

Use body language: Stand tall, look as if you mean business, speak firmly, maintain eye contact, ooze authority.

Although shorter individuals, specifically women, are often the target of aggressive domination by established parrots in the home, it is unclear how much of that abuse is related to height factors. I suspect that much of the abuse against humans by parrots may be in response to body language perceived by the

---

T-Perch Training

Although I have seen actual harm done by straight perch "stick training" and have always found it best to pet and massage birds until they are mesmerized for taming, this "touching technique" requires a practiced and experienced hand. A frequently employed alternative is T-Perch Training. This method has been described by Dr. Joachim Steinbacher, long-time editor of *Die Gefiederte Welt*, the hundred-year-old German aviculture magazine, and may be used even on birds with untrimmed wings.

The T-shaped perch should have a slightly irregular, not splintered, surface. Approach the bird slowly from the side—never pointing the perch directly at the bird. Speak gently and reassuringly to calm and inspire the bird's trust, and press the perch softly against its abdomen near the feet.

This technique requires good timing, much repetition, patience, and kindness; but there is seldom opportunity for harm to the bird, and a diligent trainer will be rewarded with a tame bird.

Left: A well-socialized bird learns to play alone happily. Right: A bird with a well-reinforced step up response will raise its foot if you say "step up" from across the room.

bird to be provocative. Waving hands and moving the head when talking, quick defensive movements, poking at the bird, and indecisive commands can easily be interpreted as invitations to bite.

Reprimand fairly: Respond appropriately to bites or other undesirable behavior. Correct a biting bird that is sitting on the hand by wobbling the hand it is sitting on, screaming "don't" or "stop" (the strong consonants are important), dropping the bird to the floor, giving the bird "time out" in an undesirable location (the bathtub), or demonstrating displaced aggression (clapping hands or slapping a rolled newspaper on a knee or table).

I like the notion of "birdlike" responses. A person with long fingernails can sometimes administer a quick pinch on the neck (just where a parrot's offended mate might nip).

In extreme cases, such as a bruising or gashing bite by a hand-fed baby that knows better, this might be the perfect time to pull a broken tail feather. I never pull feathers merely for cosmetic reasons; this painful act done without reason can destroy the trust you have worked so hard to build. But if a bird who knows better bestows great pain, I feel the appropriately timed pulling of a feather is the most severe, birdlike form of punishment acceptably administered by a human.

Return the bird to the cage only if you know that is not what it wants. Returning a biting bird to the cage may unwittingly reinforce the biting pattern.

Reprimand quickly: Timing is most important. If the response is not immediate, the bird will not understand what generated the response.

Don't shake your finger in an angry parrot's face: This is an invitation to fight or a threat to terminate the current behavior. If you must point at the bird, do it with confidence and authority. Be ready to follow through with discipline—aerobics, displaced aggression, or sensory deprivation—if necessary (see page 79). The less superfluous body language, the more clear your message of authority will be.

Don't hit the bird: As previously stated, this could excite further anger or cause injury to the bird, as well as set a poor example of the use of violence.

To spray or not to spray: There are those who use a stream of water directed at the breast along with stern words and eye contact as a last resort with very aggressive types of birds such as macaws and Amazons. I recommend the use of water exclusively as a nutrient and a reward, for frequent drenching showers are an excellent natural way for a bird to release energy that might otherwise come out as aggression. The stress caused by confusion between water, the punishment, and water, the reward, can cause feather chewing, screaming, or increased aggression—particularly in shy species.

A bird's mood can sometimes be

controlled with the power of suggestion. Because parrots often understand the phrases "good bird" and "bad bird," a misbehaving bird may immediately mellow if told "Be a good bird."

Getting comfortable with the dominant social role will enable you to handle your parrot even during raging hormone attacks. Paco is smart enough to understand that there are rules and customs to be honored and love and fun to be shared. Don't let the bird decide to make up the rules.

A word of caution: we are not dealing with a dog here. A parrot is substantially more emotional and must be allowed personal space from time to time to express those emotions. If the bird is occasionally in a really bad mood and doesn't want to be meddled with, don't intrude. Most companion parrots have a "bedtime" in the evening after which they are always cranky or downright truculent. Let them go to bed. Most companion parrots don't like to be handled when they are eating. Let them eat! If the bird appears always to be in a bad mood, then a health check and planned training program might be in order, but a sensitive human also learns to respect and allow a bird's occasional bad mood.

Chapter 3

Developing Behavior Patterns

How a Parrot Learns Behavior

The first and favorite way for a parrot to learn is by imitation. Webster's Dictionary of the English Language tells us that the verb "to parrot" means "to repeat words or actions mechanically…"

The education of a young parrot involves copying behavior from parents, siblings, and cousins who comprise the basic social unit (the flock) and receiving emotional or physical reward for successfully imitating their behavior. In the wild, successful parrot behavior is rewarded first with survival, and then, among other things, a

Two baby Amazons modeling human talking skills.

full belly. If a parrot encounters a situation for which it has learned no successful way to act, it will do whatever comes naturally—usually scream or fly away.

In the home, parrots also imitate their companions, avian or mammal. Although behavior is learned in the same way, skills needed in the living room differ from the skills needed in the field or forest. A wild bird must be able to find food and water, avoid predators, and communicate with and find the flock. A bird that strays far from the flock (actually or behaviorally) may not live to see the sunset. Skills required for happy adjustment in the home include healthy eating habits, nonviolence, self-confidence, self-sufficiency, and appropriate communication.

If there is no opportunity to copy behavior, the bird will improvise behavior to achieve the desired result. If the bird cannot fly away, it has limited options. If, for example, a parrot does not want to be held by a person with a mustache, the bird might bite every person with a mustache. If every person with a mustache who is bitten puts the bird down, this reinforces the habit of biting people with mustaches. Any behavior that is reinforced can become a pattern. If a bird establishes a pattern of biting under certain circumstances, that pattern can easily be transferred to other circumstances.

As we will discuss frequently, over 90 percent of the wild parrot's time and energy is spent foraging for and consuming food. In a captive environment, the provision of food creates an enormous void in the bird's physical and mental "habitat."

In captivity the need to fill the behavioral void created by removing the need to forage is the source of many other behaviors. These activities that take the place of other "natural" behaviors are called displacement behaviors. They can work to the bird's advantage—for example, learning healthy play habits and learning to accept a variety of foods. They can work to the bird's detriment, as when feather chewing, screaming, or roaming behaviors fill the bird's waking hours.

For a healthy social environment for a parrot, the bird should eat with its flock. I see many—sometimes severe and diverse—behavior problems in individual companon parrots that are visually isolated from the flock (human) eating area. A single bird that cannot watch other creatures eat will often develop unhealthy behavior patterns such as feather chewing, anorexia, compulsive eating, food slinging, hyperactivity, depression, or—most commonly—screaming.

It is easy for a bored companion parrot to learn to eat too much. It is just as easy for the bird to develop a desire to control the food environment by eating only one or two favored foods and pointedly rejecting all others—maybe by throwing them across the room. A bird might learn to demand extreme rituals in the offering of food.

Modeling Behaviors After Different Species

It is not unusual for the first words acquired by a new baby parrot in the home to be the names of other pets or children being called in the parent's voice. Baby parrots of one species raised in the company of other types of birds will often acquire the behaviors of those birds. It is not unusual to find an African gray parrot that speaks "conure talk" or a macaw that screams in "cockatoo."

One especially amusing case of baby parrots modeling after another species involved baby cockatiels that modeled after an orange-winged Amazon. There is a behavior often engaged in by orange-winged and mealy Amazons, and less often by other Amazons, that I call "shadowboxing." It involves striking a rigid pose—wings held out stiffly at shoulders, feathers smooth except on head and neck, flared tail, and pinpointing eyes—combined with slowly raising the head, then striking down with head and beak. Head and neck feathers are held upright in an almost circular crest—a shorter version of the crest of the hawk-headed parrot.

My friend Terry is the human companion of an orange-winged Amazon named Chappa who practices her shadowboxing daily. In typical orange-wing fashion Chappa keeps the "invisible menace" under control. At one time Terry was busy raising her first clutch of baby cockatiels, hand-feeding them in an aquarium beside Chappa's play area. Although today's domestic cockatiel is a long way from the Australian grasslands, it is a true parrot, with the strong characteristic tendency to copy behavior. When I visited one morning, all four baby cockatiels were intently imitating this orange-wing shadowboxing behavior— neck feathers straight out, wings extended stiffly, fiercely stabbing an invisible enemy.

The most common behavior successfully imitated by parrots from other species is the production of sounds. Modeling is particularly valuable in teaching baby parrots to talk. Although a parrot can improvise

A large parrot who watches humans eat with utensils may—with patience—learn to eat with a spoon.

screaming, it must have a teacher to learn words. The motivation to copy behavior of companions is a significant reason that birds learn speech more readily from humans than from tape recorders.

A companion hookbill can also learn to scream by the model of humans arguing or calling to each other in loud voices. Only a few parrots have such a strong innate tendency to scream that problematic screaming develops on it's own. A true screaming problem is usually reinforced, although the reinforcement is usually unintentional and often takes the form of isolation and/or neglect. As we will discuss further, almost any interaction—or lack of interaction—with a parrot might reinforce the bird's behavior.

Since several types of parrots do have a strong tendency to develop a screaming problem, a caring and conscientious bird owner carefully teaches them not to scream. Modeling is an excellent way to teach a bird not to scream. Cockatoo aficionado Debbie Kesling uses a technique that she calls the "contact call." Rather than allowing the bird to establish a pattern of loud screaming to determine where its companion is, the bird is shown how to call or whistle softly back and forth with a companion who is out of sight. It is easier to model a pattern like this in a home where a quiet contact call occurs naturally.

Unintentional modeling often combines with unintentional reinforcement to form behavor patterns. It is harder to model quiet calls in a home with boisterous dogs and children who must be called from outside. Failure by humans to understand that they are setting an example that will be copied by their baby parrot can lead to the development of many surprising and problematic behaviors. For example, a baby parrot who has its beak customarily grabbed, even in the friendliest way, will soon be grabbing people by the beaks (noses). The response that baby bird receives to this behavior can be quite confusing. That same person who taught the baby to grab "noses" might be the first to reprimand the bird for copying that behavior. This do-as-I-say-not-as-I-do scenario is just as confounding to a bird as it is to human children. I find the modeling of confusing behavior to baby parrots is often observed in the presence of inexplicable and dysfunctional behavior on the part of the bird.

Enhancing the Motivation to Copy Behavior

It has been demonstrated—both inside and outside the laboratory—that the motivation to copy behaviors can be enhanced by providing a competitive situation in which the bird learns. This technique has been extensively studied by Dr. Irene Pepperberg in her work with African gray parrots. The rival may be a competitor of the same or a different species, as when one teaches a companion bird to speak by rewarding a human rival for speaking an appropriate word or phrase. I have seen effective use of a rival to stimulate learning in older human-bonded birds as well as younger ones. (See "The Gray Parrot Who Wouldn't Talk" on page 140.) A parrot learning to speak with a teacher/rival system is just as likely to learn to speak in the voice of the rival as that of the teacher.

The Effects of Environment on Companion Parrot Behavior

Training, a favored tool in dog behavior management, is also instrumental in good companion parrot behavior; but a balanced environment is the easiest, most natural way to a happily adjusted bird. Height, cage, territory, location, light, accessories, and access to appropriate choices have undeniable influence on the development of acceptable behaviors. Manipulating these elements can usually prevent and sometimes correct common behavior problems.

Training a few elementary behaviors such as stepping onto a hand or perch and acclimating to restraint for veterinary examination are important for quality life. However, many of the benefits of aggression-prevention training for parrots come from the training of humans to use authoritative, yet not threatening nor provocative mannerisms.

While training is important, I believe environment has equal influence on happy behavioral adjustment in companion parrots. Even a well-trained hookbill may develop serious behavior problems if denied an adequate environment. During many years of helping people and their birds to understand each other I have seen quite a few pleasant, charming, well-behaved parrots who had no training whatsoever. Their owners have—often intuitively—provided an environment that prevented the development of the "big three" problems—screaming, biting, and feather chewing.

Height

Whether the parrot looks up or down at a housemate influences how the bird will interact with that person and can be instrumental in the development of aggression. A normal parrot maintaining the pecking order in its home environment will usually be sweet, friendly, and cooperative with humans at whom it looks up and may be threatening or nippy toward any creature—man, woman, dog or cat—upon whom it looks down.

This is often observed in public places where humans are allowed to handle large parrots. It is not coincidental that a pet shop with waist-high perches has sweeter, more tolerant birds than a shop housing birds above eye level.

Height can also sometimes compensate for fearfulness in companion birds. Startling behavioral changes

have been brought about by either lowering "mean" birds or raising "shy" ones. For effective behavior management, some birds must be housed with their eyes lower than shorter humans' mouths; and some birds will respond dependably to handling by any human only when spending time at waist height. I have seen some very truculent birds respond with surprising sweetness to being housed for a time on the floor.

Cage/Space

A bird needs a spacious, easy-to-climb cage. I see a correlation between the amount of space a parrot occupies and the ferocity with which it seeks to control that space. The influence of space on behavior is particularly observable in the case of African grays and macaws, either of which can be unfavorably affected by a poorly planned environment. I disagree completely with avian writers who say that macaws make poor pets after the age of two, nor do I feel that macaws require any more "training" than an Amazon or gray parrot. In the presence of a well-reinforced step-up response, good conditioning to restraint, cooperation for flapping exercises, and aggression-prevention mannerisms by human companions, I believe that a macaw in a well-planned environment requires no more time nor attention than, for example, a yellow nape. On the other hand, a macaw requires considerably *more* environment than a yellow nape.

I think a bird needs a cage at least one and a half times its untrimmed wing span in at least two, but preferably, three dimensions. That is, if the bird has a two-foot (.6 m) wing span, the cage where the bird spends the majority of its time needs to be at least three feet (1 m) tall, three feet (1 m) wide, and three feet (1 m) deep.

If space is marginal or barely adequate, behavior might be enhanced by manipulating the bird's perception of space. For example, it is not a good idea to take an established companion bird from a larger cage and place it directly into a permanent smaller cage. If a lifestyle change dictates that the bird must go to a smaller cage, it is best kept in an even smaller cage for a few weeks, then introduced to the new cage which will now seem larger.

One of my favorite examples of manipulation of perceived space is a piece of Chris Davis advice from years ago. It seems that a particular bird would scream "all the time" if it was not allowed to sit on top of its cage. The owner was unable to allow the bird that much liberty, so Chris recommended a cage within a much larger cage. The bird could sit on top of the inner cage yet remain restrained; presumably the bird would have the feeling of being outside "the" cage and would, therefore, discontinue screaming.

A parrot with a well-appointed cage is never bored.

Territory

Spending too much time in one place can lead to the development of aggression. Monitor and modify the development of territorial aggression with a well-planned captive environment, including a "roost" and multiple "foraging" areas. In the wild, most parrots sleep in approximately the same place every night (unless they are actually nesting). Every day they forage in several areas where there might be a newly maturing food source; a past-its-prime field to be scoured for leftovers; a known dependable source of minerals or insects; a shallow pool for bathing; a cool, shady place for an afternoon nap; or a couple of potential new haunts for investigation.

A "home bird" forced to remain in exactly the same place day after day will often come to guard that space so aggressively that no one can service the cage or even walk by without a feigned, attempted, or successful attack. The provision of multiple "foraging" areas within the home will minimize this behavior by enlarging the perceived "territory." One might provide several fixed-location bird-proof areas or one portable play area to be moved from room to room. A bird who enjoys multiple play or foraging areas requires less sleeping cage space than a bird who remains in or on the cage most of the time. For optimal result, the sleeping cage is placed far from foraging areas.

Just as a bird who spends too much time in one place becomes possessively defensive of that territory, a bird who spends too much time with one human possessively defends that "human territory." Occasional visits outside the home, particularly with less-than-favorite humans, lessen the ill effects of immoderate bonds to perceived territory, including "human territory." Since a young bird may bond—at least initially—to a favorite human in a territorial manner, excursions out of the home with less-than-favorite humans will support a balanced relationship between the companion bird and all humans in the home (the flock).

Location

In addition to the influences of height, space, and territory, the location of a companion parrot's space plays a role in social adjustment. Common and predictable screaming behaviors can easily be stimulated by actual or perceived isolation from "the flock" or the flock's activities. Perceived isolation might be something as simple as the bird's inability to see people when they go around a corner (add a mirror, possibly one of those convex "shoplifter" mirrors) or inability to see what everyone else is watching (be sure the bird can see the television, or it might go crazy trying to figure out what everyone else is watching). Of course, actual isolation in a basement or back room is the worst thing to do to a bird screaming from a feeling of isolation.

I also see biting behaviors in quite a few birds who must be frequently

rushed past because of a cage located in the epicenter of what might be a daily "earthquake" — the fixing of breakfast and hustling children off to school or the home-protection efforts of a couple of boisterous dogs. Sometimes moving a cage only a few feet can minimize this effect. For example, a bird area that must, because of space limitations, be on either side of a busy doorway might elicit better bird behavior on one side of the doorway rather than the other. Behavioral benefits from the move might be derived because the people or dogs customarily rush in what is now a relatively different direction or because the bird has better near vision on one side than the other.

Light and Light Periods

When evaluating a particular bird's environment, attention must be paid to the quality and amount of light the bird receives. Required amount of full-spectrum light and length of daylight periods probably vary with each type of bird. A bird who receives too little light or low-quality light may be poorly feathered, inactive, overweight, and may fail to vocalize. This is sometimes accompanied by low thyroid output, which may or may not be coincidental. An outdoor cage situated to provide for and protect from direct sunlight contributes to both good health and good behavior.

A bird receiving too much light might exhibit hypersexuality, irritability, screaming, biting, and feather chewing. A person seeking to normalize a particular bird's environment might investigate light periods in the bird's native range, altering the length of light periods for behavioral effect. Light periods are often manipulated to commence or terminate breeding, to modify lethargy, obesity, hypersexuality, aggression, screaming, self-mutilation, and failure to talk.

Accessories

No environmental examination can be complete without an evaluation of accessories—chewing, ringing, holding, climbing, swinging, preening, and "bopping" toys. The easiest, least expensive, and most accessible of these are tree branches with bark. Branches with bark help keep beak and toenails appropriately worn and help prevent foot problems and numerous behavioral problems. I like ailanthus or sumac branches.

Loro Parque in the Canary Islands provides fresh pine branches weekly. I think most taller trees are probably safe. I consider all shrubs, fruit trees, and trees that might have been sprayed with chemicals to be potentially toxic. Clean and examine branches for bugs.

Every bird should have several choices of commonly favored bird activities, such as ringing a bell, preening a fuzzy pseudo-friend, climbing both fixed and swinging objects, and "bopping" a fleeting, shiny reflection. Sometimes a particular toy will hang in the cage for quite some time before the bird learns how to play with it. Sometimes a toy will be ignored for long periods only to be discovered as a favorite buddy. A well rounded hookbill should probably have at least a half dozen toys, some of which are routinely withheld and returned to reinforce good behavior or distract from anticipated bad behavior.

Many active, well-behaved, kind-to-humans parrots have daily play rituals that involve "beating up" or otherwise physically dominating a toy. Just because a bird abuses a toy doesn't mean that it will abuse humans. In fact, like frequent drenching showers, abuse of toys releases energy that might otherwise emerge as aggression against humans.

Access to Appropriate Choices

A happy hookbill needs many opportunities for good behavior and few opportunities for bad behavior. For

example, a bird sitting on the shoulder has several choices of things to do—chew on buttons, moles, jewelry, eyeglasses, or earlobes; make holes in fabric or preen hair. For various reasons, none of these choices is perceived by humans as appropriate behavior.

For better or worse, human responses usually—often unintentionally—reinforce a bird's behavior. If

A well-designed companion parrot environment should include many things for the bird to chew. This gives it ready access to approved behaviors and little or no access to unapproved behaviors.

behavior is largely dependent upon the willingness of humans to modify their own behavior or accommodate environmental changes required to stimulate better behavior in the bird.

Humans often constitute the only "flock" after which the bird can pattern its behavior. Under the modeling of an angry—or even a passively angry—owner, a bird can easily learn violent behavior. If humans in the environment taunt or ignore the bird, if they taunt or ignore each other, a companion parrot can easily develop undesirable or antisocial behaviors. It is not unusual for owners of a good talking type of bird that is not talking to admit that humans do not talk to each other in their home.

Long Term Adjustment

We don't always get along with every life companion all the time; and there will be times when "parrot stew" sounds very tempting. New behaviors will develop from time to time, and no bird is going to behave perfectly all the time. I believe, however, that ongoing evaluation and manipulation of the environment is just as important as training for an easy-to-live-with, longtime companion parrot.

Achieving Verbal Communication With a Parrot

Even while it is still inside the egg, a baby parrot may verbally communicate its need for the parents to provide

the bird has little or no opportunity for inappropriate behavior, the human interaction will usually be reinforcing acceptable behavior. In a poorly planned environment a bird owner can wind up yelling "No" all the time. This can be quite amusing to a bird who loves *any* attention or damaging to a bird with low self-confidence.

A bird with several exciting things to do will not need to chew on treasured furniture. In a well-planned environment, the bird has no unsupervised access to inappropriate choices. Ideally, access to that tasty-looking basket collection is restricted with physical barriers, psychological barriers, and/or wing feather trims.

People are, undoubtedly, the most influential part of the companion parrot's environment as they stimulate, provoke, and reinforce the bird's behavior, as well as provide for the physical elements of the environment. The ability to modify a companion bird's food and care. Failure to do so, especially just after hatching, results in death by neglect—swift elimination of nonverbal babies from the gene pool. This natural selection process ensures an adult individual who can find its mate and flock when separated, communicate safety, alarm, and an unknown number of other messages to its peers.

Although much remains to be learned about why, how, and what parrots communicate verbally, we know that their ability to verbalize is not limited to communication in their own language—that they can and do learn other animal languages as well as human language. Studies done by Dr. Irene Pepperberg with African gray parrots are particularly startling, revealing even an ability to understand numbers.

Those who live with talking pets spend many happy hours exchanging stories about profound words from feathered friends. These "talking-bird people" are surprisingly like their parrots—highly communicative, frequently possessing exaggerated verbal tendencies. Like all effective communicators, they take the time to talk to friends, family, and birds.

I believe that verbal communication skills are an important step in achieving an effective relationship with a parrot. It is possible and important to relate verbally to birds both through human speech and through their own language.

Birds spend a large portion of their lives scolding, chattering, and singing to each other. They bill and coo, scream and curse. They are particularly verbal in territorial disputes, but even when comfortable in their own space, they are famous for generating great volumes of sound (some people even call it noise). They are most likely to try to communicate verbally when separated from their "flock" —when they can hear, but not see their companions. To establish a verbally interactive human/avian relationship, begin by trying to understand and respond to the bird's sounds.

Speak the bird's language: When you spend time with a "prespeech" bird, there are certain sounds it makes when presented with particular stimuli. An African gray may "click" when it sees that favorite toy on the floor. A budgie or Amazon may "trill" to the hair dryer or "tut, tut, tut, tut" to the reflection in the mirror. If you can reproduce the situation by making the same sound as the bird, then enticing the bird to repeat the sound, you have made a major communication breakthrough. You have modeled a behavior for the bird, then stimulated the bird to mimic the behavior.

Tell stories: A companion bird loves to be entertained with stories —particularly if it hears its own name in that story. "Once upon a time, there was a pudgy, green Amazon named Portia. One day, when Portia was only a naked nestling, he fell from the tree where his mother had laid him...."

A bird that stretches a friendly greeting probably also will be motivated to try to communicate vocally.

It may not really matter what words come between the "Portia's," but a steady stream of words in a friendly tone, freely interspersed with the bird's name will capture its curiosity and establish direct, personal communication.

Be redundant: A companion parrot will usually pick up the word it hears most frequently, usually, a greeting. "Hello" in English is sometimes a little difficult for a bird to master, so try the Spanish greeting, "Hola," (pronounced "Oh la"), or the more continental "Ciao," (pronounced "Chow"). Birds usually repeat single-syllable greetings first—"What," "Hi," Ciao,"—followed later by "Hello" and "What' cha doin'?"

After the greeting, the next most frequently repeated word in the household is often the name of a child or another pet. Yellow napes are famous for making everybody crazy by calling children or other pets in the mother's voice. They love "itty" sounds, like "pretty bird" and "itty, bitty, pretty one." A large number of talking companion parrots say "Here, Kitty, Kitty, Kitty."

Portia, my yellow nape, greets the doorbell with "Hello" and answers a knock with "Come in." I once encountered him repeating "Hello" in a strange, almost frantic manner. First he said "Hello" in his greeting voice, then "Hello?" questioningly, then "Hello! Hello!" angrily. He then repeated the sequence. Upon investigation, I found him watching a TV game show that included a bell similar to my doorbell. He appeared frustrated that whoever was ringing that bell would not respond to him! Unlike a dog barking at a dog on television — a natural response in the dog's own language — Portia was making a learned response to a stimulus and making that response with learned sounds, to him a "foreign" language.

Be conversant: While some parrots merely repeat individual words, others repeat whole or partial conversations, and they do so at surprisingly appropriate moments. They may say "Hi," pause for response, then "Whatcha doin'?" when you come home; "Bye," pause and "Take it easy," when you leave; "Come here" when they want you to come over; "What!" when frightened; and "Night, Night!" when it's time for bed.

I know a young Timneh African gray owner who lives downstairs from his mom. The bird repeats a frequent conversation between mother and son that goes something like this:

Mom's voice: "Clark?"

Son's voice: "What?"

Mom's voice: "Mumble, mumble, mumble."

Son's voice: "Okay."

The bird garbles the variable words but reproduces the tone and cadence of the mother's voice recognizably.

Set a talkative example: A young parrot that is not talked to or spends all its time with birds or humans who don't talk to each other will have less of a desire to communicate verbally.

Baby babble: Baby parrots get the cadence down first. They usually mutter unrecognizable syllables and practice babbling for hours, sometimes quietly and sometimes loudly before actually producing understandable words.

The riff (or roll): Every day, most healthy, talking parrots will spend a noticeable amount of time repeating what seems like their full repertoire of words. If a word disappears from its usual position in the sequence, it may not be heard again. Usually, however, the word will reappear later. In the instance of very intelligent species, I believe the dropped word does not require daily use but is learned sufficiently to be called forth when the occasion arises.

Cooing: Soothing "OOOOO" sounds are helpful when wishing to calm an angry, upset, or frightened bird. Totally wild or totally tame, all our feathered friends love lots of "Pooor, baaby" and "Pooor, pooor birdie."

Hissssssing: On the other hand, most birds will become alerted or even frightened by "shhh" or other hissing noises that sound like their natural enemy, the snake. Indeed, many birds—even nestlings—make snakelike hissing sounds themselves to ward off other creatures. Hissing or shushing at the bird can make it nervous and negatively affect its health and behavior.

Singing: Whether you want your bird's undivided attention or wish to express joy to your bird, nothing is quite as effective as song. Many birds are totally mesmerized by singing humans, and others will court or sing along. Even if you are just "hanging out" with the bird, it will appreciate your song just as much as you enjoy the bird's song. I do not usually recommend the good-talking Amazons (*Amazona ochrocephala*) to voice students, as these birds will aggressively interfere with practice.

Whispering: Sometimes, particularly in dealing with a screamer, the most effective way to get the bird's attention is by whispering. This behavior communicates to the bird that its screams have been heard. If you cannot understand why it is screaming or are unable to change whatever it's screaming about, at least you are modeling an appropriate method of getting attention. If the bird is a "quick study," it might catch on and try whispering for your attention next time.

Scolding: In relating to birds, birdlike behaviors are most effective, and scolding is an absolutely birdlike behavior. If there are 20 or more birds in a tree, odds are that at least one bird is giving another bird a piece of its mind. Strong, sharp consonants are more effective as verbal reprimands: "Don't" or "Stop" rather than "No," which may sound almost soothing if not delivered with force.

To whistle or not to whistle: Some people contend that if one teaches a good-talking bird to whistle, it will not reach its full talking potential. It seems that since a bird has no vocal cords, speech is accomplished by "moving" the lining of the bifurcated trachea into different configurations while expelling air across that opening. Therefore, a talking parrot is actually "whistling" in syllables, and true whistling is more natural and easier to accomplish than talking. Types of parrots with a propensity for mimicking appear to have good control over the musculature in the trachea. Types of parrots with poor talking potential may have an inefficiently shaped trachea or poor control over the muscles of the trachea.

A very good talker might occasionally become so enchanted with a new whistle that it will discontinue talking in favor of whistling for a time. It happened to my young yellow nape when a well-meaning friend taught him to wolf whistle. Portia didn't talk for a couple of weeks, and nearly drove me mad with that obnoxious whistle.

I don't think it's a bad idea, however, to use whistling as a substitute or a transition for teaching birds who find talking difficult or for birds, such as the female cockatiel, in whom speech is considered very difficult. Many parrots that may be only fair talkers can become accomplished whistlers. I know quite a few who loudly entertain with "London Bridge," "Colonel Bogie March," or "Beethoven's Fifth" at any opportunity.

Don't scream: It is very easy to teach most parrots to scream. This is an instinctive reaction to visual isolation and barrier frustration and is easily reinforced by screaming back and forth from one room to another. Also, no matter how loudly a bird screams—particularly if it is a good

Sweet Talk

Probably the most emotional thing my bird ever said to me was not intentionally taught to him. I had to leave Portia with friends for a few months while I dealt with personal matters. Portia never understood why I had abandoned him. He called my name and cried for me in a human voice, but whenever I went to see him, he was speechless.

The couple with whom he was staying worked opposite shifts for the same company. When one of them was at home and the other at work, they talked on the phone. Sometimes they talked about business, sometimes not; but they called each other often.

It was wonderful to finally bring Portia home. He was thrilled and absolutely in awe, so being the very good bird, he was perfectly quiet the first day. The morning of the second day, however, he got excited when I vacuumed around his cage. Portia fanned his tail, strutted around the top of the cage and "pinpointed" his eyes in the manner of talking Amazons. When I turned off the vacuum cleaner, he strutted over to the edge of the cage, stretched out as far as possible in full display, and said, in a slightly nasty voice, "Well, why didn't you call me back!"

I felt it was the closest he could come to "Why did you leave me over there so long." I held him in my arms and tried to explain all the things I had to take care of and why he couldn't be with me; then he seemed content.

The couple he stayed with acknowledged that he had heard those words only once. That was many years ago, and to my knowledge he has never repeated that sentence. This incident made me aware that some birds can verbally communicate very subtle feelings—love, longing, even a concept of time—effectively in human speech.

talker—don't try to reprimand it by screaming back. You might be teaching another loud call to practice at sunrise. Better to deliver a stern look and a forceful reprimand in a calm, assertive voice followed by some form of distraction (exercise, bathing, or toys).

Use Words in Context/Avoid Recordings: If you want a bird to merely mimic, a recording might be the most effective way to accomplish that objective. I believe, however, that the potential for damage is greater than the perceived benefits. Having to listen to the same 20 seconds of material over and over can stress the bird and contribute to screaming, unexplained aggression, self-mutilation, or intellectual withdrawal.

In contrast, a bird taught to use words in context is more likely to use them at appropriate times in appropriate situations. Can you imagine being taught to make sounds that don't mean anything? I believe that using words the bird can say to represent their meaning enhances and stimulates the bird's motivation to speak.

Don't Talk Dirty: Responsible owners understand that their parrots will outlive them, and they avoid teaching profanity. A bird with a dirty mouth might have a hard time finding a home when you're gone. Of course, they always seem to pick up just what we don't want them to say! The children of the widow on my block found out about mom's new boyfriend when the budgie started saying, "Kiss me quick behind the door"!

Don't become discouraged if it seems to take a long time for the bird to learn to speak your language. It is an awesome accomplishment for any creature. I have seen birds who never managed a single word speak up to 20 words four years after their introduction to the home.

It is a parrot's nature to communicate verbally. Even if your bird is not fluent in your language, keep listening. I'm sure it is trying to tell you something.

Stimulating the Reluctant Talker

Different types of parrots are known to have differing propensities for mimicking human speech. The ease with which a parrot can physically produce speech is probably determined by the musculature in the trachea. Sound is produced by expelling air across the mouth of the bifurcated trachea. Variations in the sound are produced when the bird alters the "depth" and shape of the trachea. Some parrots such as the African gray parrot seem to have great ability to produce various sounds while others such as the cockatiel have limited ability to produce varied sounds. There is also great variation between individuals of the same type. A good-talking cockatiel might have a larger vocabulary than a poor-talking African gray.

A well-socialized, home-bred baby parrot often learns to talk more quickly than a human infant. It is somewhat more difficult to stimulate a wild-caught bird to learn to communicate verbally with human speech.

In addition to physical propensity, a parrot must be motivated to communicate. I believe parrots who rapidly narrow the pupil of their eyes ("pinpointing" or "flashing") are demonstrating a high level of interest in whatever is going on, including verbal communication. Frequent pinpointing is often observed in good-talking parrots, and I believe lack of or infrequent pinpointing can be an indication of either poor health or poor motivation.

Talking ability in parrots is unrelated to disposition. Some of the orneriest, meanest, most aggressive birds I have ever seen were great talk-ers. Many of the environmental manipulations we use to stimulate a reluctant talker are also those we use to reduce aggression. A balance must be maintained so that the bird is happy and excited about life, but not arrogant and temperamental enough to abuse humans.

Presuming a particular bird is of a type known to be capable of human speech, the following will help stimulate the nontalking parrot to speech.

• Include the bird in your daily rituals like showering, grooming (be careful with aerosols) and eating. Allow the bird to observe you sleeping and expressing affection. Participating in or observing these activities replicates the feeling of being a part of the flock and there

A pinpointing eye movement is a sign of excitement or interest. It may indicate motivation to talk or to bite.

will be a natural instinct to desire communication with other members of the flock.

- If the bird is usually housed lower than eye level and there is little problem with aggression, allow it to spend some social time in a very high place. The intoxication of height might stimulate aggression, screaming, or in a shy bird, speech.

- If the bird seems to suffer from poor self-esteem but is acclimated to the home environment, try allowing it a little more wing feather than usual when grooming; or perhaps allow the wing feathers to grow in completely to stimulate the motivation to communicate.

- Role model for the bird by calling back and forth with a human companion. Talk to the bird as you would to a human baby, using words to represent their meaning. Put a human companion in a competitive situation where the human companion receives a reward that the bird wants for speaking an easy-to-say word like "What."

- Try to provide a like species role model to teach the bird to talk. (See "The Gray Parrot Who Wouldn't Talk," page 140.) If you can't find a role model, try establishing a rival or competitive student.

- Try to learn the meaning of a particular sound the bird uses; then use it with the same meaning.

- Try allowing access to a "bird-safe mirror"—a flat piece of shiny metal that swings on a chain. Watch out for the development of aggression around the bird mirror.

- Many birds find it fun to talk "into" the corner or the seed dish. Give the bird an interesting "echo" device in it's cage, maybe a jar, metal can, or plastic cup.

- Watch lots of Tarzan movies and nature programs. Yell at television sports activities, in bird screams if possible.

- Stand out of sight of the bird and whistle. Try to get the bird to whistle back.

- Make up stories that mention the bird's name frequently. Sing to the bird when you run the shower, dishwasher, or vacuum cleaner.

- Establish singing, dancing, or music rituals: vacuum to "William Tell Overture," shower to "The Thieving Magpie," or perform Brigadoon on Sunday mornings.

- Participate in passive games such as "Blink" and "Peep-eye," (see page 18).

- Most importantly, if there are several people in the household, *talk to each other* as well as to the bird.

Chapter 4

Domestic Hand-fed Parrots

Avoiding the Hand-fed Baby Blues

Marathon cuddling is a great way to befriend an older parrot or new import, but it may be the worst possible thing for a newly weaned hand-fed baby. It is not easy to live with a determined parrot that requires constant attention. To understand this behavior and how to prevent it, let's look at the psychological development of the baby bird.

A baby bird doesn't seek food like a kitten or puppy. The primary instinct of a new hatchling is to beg to attract parents to feed. From its first moments, the codependent creature must persuade others to do all work involved in its survival.

By weaning time, begging has been honed to a fine, noisy art. Just saying "no" to the demanding youngsters is incredibly stressful to parents. A wild daddy bird weaning babies looks like a prisoner trying to escape. If the babies see him, they will chase and beg, chase and beg until the ex-

hausted daddy just sits there surrounded by screaming birds that may be virtually indistinguishable from him except by behavior.

A baby parrot bonded to humans learns to demand cuddling as well as food. Typically, humans might even argue over whose turn it is to hold an adorable baby parrot. A newly acquired hand-fed might be held, cuddled, and nurtured literally every waking hour.

Most families cannot afford to provide a human to hold the bird for its entire 30-to-80-year lifetime. Behavior problems appear at about the time humans decide they might like to do something other than hold the bird all the time. It may be one of those cruel quirks of fate that the "terrible twos" arrives at about this time, but the behavior problems are not coincidental. An undisciplined juvenile has a more difficult period of adjustment ahead than a well-trained one.

In addition to the amount of time the baby bird is nurtured, the quality of that nurturing also plays an important role in the bird's social development. The emotional chemistry generated when one's favorite bundle of feathers puffs up and cheeps with contentment into a human neck or cheek can be almost frightening. A young bird soaks up effusive praise and affection like a sponge. Although intermittent reinforcement simply for not engaging in negative behaviors is an important element in raising a well-behaved parrot, constant reinforcement for nothing at all can produce a bird that is addicted to praise and affection, that will violently demand what it expects, and may literally attack the "abandoning" human.

The begging posture in a newly weaned macaw.

A juvenile bird just past weaning showered with excessive human affection and having every avian demand instantly provided will expect humans to be physical and emotional slaves and will often learn to bite to obtain special treatment.

An over-nurtured (spoiled) parrot may be hyperactive; scream for attention; refuse to go back to the cage; bite when attention is paid to other pets, people, or the telephone; or simply chew its feathers off. An overly protected parrot might become timorous, terrified of all unfamiliar people, places, and things. Probably the bird will manipulate its adoring family by pretending fear of something. For example, a bird that wants to be held all the time might exhibit great fear when asked to sit on a perch (any designed-for-a-bird sitting place).

I see many 18-month old parrots, particularly cockatoos and macaws, on the brink of homelessness be-

cause they are driving family members crazy by demanding constant attention. These "hand-fed baby blues" can be avoided as follows:

1. *Don't hold the newly weaned baby all the time.* Establish a daily or weekly schedule that is no more than 20 percent of the amount of time you reasonably expect to spend holding the bird the rest of its life. Keep a log, if necessary, to ensure that the bird is not reinforced to expect constant handling. The bird must learn to play alone.

2. *Don't mollycoddle the bird.* While a baby bird's physical and emotional needs must be met, hypersensitivity to a baby's every whim will teach that it should expect to get everything it wants. This leads to temper tantrums later if every demand is not immediately met. The baby bird's need for guidance and discipline is greater than its need for instant gratification.

3. When the bird is quietly and successfully entertaining itself, *reward on an intermittent basis.*

4. *Teach appropriate behaviors.* The baby bird must dependably respond to the step-up prompt. The bird must be able to entertain itself in a safe, quiet, nondestructive way. This is largely a function of a well-planned environment. A large, secure, well-equipped cage and play area will provide both a sense of security and control. The baby bird needs many toys, puzzles, swings, ropes, and other approved items to hold its interest.

5. *Don't let the bird spend time higher than your eyes in its own territory.* This includes snuggling on the shoulder at home. If the bird has a dependable step-up response, shoulders are occasionally acceptable in a crowded or threatening public place. But at home, the access to the shoulder will contribute to the development of dominance behaviors. Keep the bird on the hand or snuggled under the chin for the following reasons:

   - It is virtually impossible to achieve eye contact and require a "step-up" response from your own shoulder. Many birds will bite or run to the middle of the back before owner authority can be reestablished. Typically, a controlling little parrot loves to see you lose control and may bite the hand before stepping up onto it.

This young macaw is barely weaned, but it already has learned to pull up a bucket for a treat.

57

- A parrot (even a cockatiel or budgie) on the shoulder may think that it is in charge of the branch (your body). Someday that bird might decide that it wants that other bird (your head) off the branch. This behavior may be a few years down the road, but for most healthy parrots, the time will come when they cannot control their bites.
6. *Provide frequent and varied nontactile entertainment* (TV, music, singing, talking, and toys).
7. *Take the bird on lots of outings and encourage interaction with unfamiliar people and objects.*

Attention-demanding behaviors in a young parrot are only part of the "terrible twos," which can arrive anytime after six months. Prevention training will lessen the impact on loving family members with understandably limited patience.

The Developmental Period Doesn't Have to Be the "Terrible Twos"

Sometime during the first year or two, the healthy, intelligent human-bonded baby parrot enters a period of emotional development that tests the limits of the companion social order and of the environment. This period is particularly pronounced in baby yellow napes, but it is observable in almost all types of Amazons, grays,

cockatoos, macaws, and conures. Even young imported parrots that have been tamed go through it. It appears roughly 6 to 15 months after weaning (in captive-raised birds) or taming (in imported birds). This period is usually more pronounced in captive-raised birds.

A parrot's developmental period is comparable to the "terrible twos" in which the human toddler says "No!" to everything. During this phase, the baby parrot may exhibit hard, deliberate biting; increased persecution of both perceived "inferiors" and almost all other members of the pecking order; changing and rechanging loyalties. It is also a time of increased curiosity and vocalization.

I receive calls from surprised humans who say that their baby parrot has "turned on them at nine months old" and that they are thinking of "getting rid" of the baby bird. I see quite a few baby macaws get bounced from home to home at about this time. It came as a big surprise to me that an owner of a very expensive bird might rather give the bird away than invest a hundred dollars and a little time and courage in behavior modification.

The duration and emotional intensity of the developmental period is favorably influenced by well-planned behavioral training. If humans have not yet initiated a system of aggression-prevention handling techniques, this can be a very difficult time for everyone. If the baby bird has been trained to the hand with the Egyptian Method (see page 22) and has a well-reinforced step-up response, both humans and bird alike will have a much easier time getting through the negative aspects of this very exciting period of emotional and intellectual growth.

If the baby bird was spoiled during or just after weaning (see pages 55–58 on "Avoiding the Hand-fed Baby Blues"), there will be much human emotional pain as Paco, Jr. manipulates humans with guilt as well as aggression. A typical scenario can go something like this:

MacPaco MacAwe, Jr., a 14-month-old juvenile blue and gold macaw, expects to be held whenever his human is in the room. The minute Mom/Dad comes home, the begging begins. There is much dancing and leaning toward Mom/Dad, eye excitement, and verbalization, including actual begging noises.

If Mom/Dad is not a "cruel and heartless monster," of course Baby will be picked up. At this point the tone of the interaction may change. Instead of being the snuggle bunny he was at six months, MacPaco, Jr. is alive with curiosity and the desire to play. Everything Mom/Dad is wearing is subject to acute investigation, stones are removed from rings, teeth are lunged for, eyeglasses are grabbed; hair, eyes, ears, and noses are tasted. When MacPaco, Jr. decides to remove the mole from Mom/Dad's neck, there is a swift "No!" and they head for the cage.

As Jr. sees the cage rapidly approaching, he decides that he will not go back. His grip on the forearm tightens, the nails dig into the flesh, he grabs the upper arm or shoulder in that awesome beak and hangs on.

Mom/Dad gets scratches on the forearm and a nasty bruise on the upper arm and drops the bird to the floor before retreating in pain to the medicine cabinet. The bird walks to its play area and climbs up on its playpen for just a little while longer.

Of course each type of parrot plays out its own version of this story. The precocious baby yellow nape may reach down and deliver a firm bite and then say "Ouch!" or "No!" and laugh.

The phobic baby gray will flap frantically and thrash about breaking wing and tail feathers.

A baby conure might "clamp down" with that sharp little beak and have to be pried off.

This doesn't mean that the bird doesn't like the owner. When the bird behavior consultant comes over, MacPaco, Jr. is perfectly behaved. The fact that the behavior is a ritualistic, repeated pattern but occurs selectively demonstrates that it is an action that can be modified rather than a reaction over which the bird has no control.

Sometimes it seems that the baby is trying to learn to do everything we are trying to keep it from learning. The reality is that it is trying to learn everything.

The age at which a bird reaches "the terrible twos" is highly variable. I think I see a correlation to the size of the bird: that smaller birds reach it sooner—maybe at 5 to 12 months —and larger birds reach it later, sometimes as late as 30 months. In some birds this phase will arrive with a vengeance; in others it may be almost imperceptible.

The key to happy present and future adjustment lies in aggression-prevention training and in exploiting the positive aspects of this developmental phase. In the wild, the juvenile bird would be learning to find food and water, learning to venture away and then rejoin the flock, and learning to avoid predators. The bird would be testing all relationships to learn its own exact status in the flock—the behavioral niche over which it has complete control.

In captivity, the young parrot will learn to climb, flap and talk or escape, destroy and scream. The role models will be human, other companion animals, or absent. Most solitary baby birds must improvise—they must figure out the limits of acceptable behavior completely on their own, without like role models. They will test the limits of acceptable behavior just for the fun of it!

At this time, the bird requires the greatest environmental stimulation of its life. Every effort should be made to provide Junior with many experiences and opportunities for initiative. Later in life, many birds will be quite content with a new toy every month. At this stage, Baby Bird should have multiple new toys at a time. This gives the bird a chance to make *appropriate* independent decisions and gives

it the feeling of having control over the environment. Having the experience and therefore the ability to make decisions will give the bird a sense of security when presented with unfamiliar circumstances or situations in the future. But toys should not be introduced insensitively. Some baby birds are afraid of new things; some baby birds love the attention they receive by *acting afraid.*

The entire environment to which the bird has access should have many opportunities for approved behaviors and few opportunities for disapproved behaviors. It is easy to wind up screaming "No!," "Don't!," or "Stop that!" almost every time you speak to the bird. Providing a bird-proofed environment gives you many opportunities to reward the bird for appropriate behaviors. It's a good time for MacPaco, Jr. to learn to climb a knotted rope, eat with a spoon, or swing in a swing (in macaws that means becoming a trapeze artist, so give them lots of space). It's a good time for speech training, so use simple words the bird can pick up to describe familiar things. You will have greater success using and repeating words in context than simply saying a word with no obvious meaning to the bird. Hand-fed baby parrots will often learn to say "No!," "Don't," "Stop that!," "Com'ere," "Hi," "Night-Night," and "Gi'mme" spontaneously at an earlier age than human infants do.

This is a prime time for the bird to learn that it can get Mom/Dad's attention by doing something bad or merely inappropriate. It is the perfect time for the hand-fed, human-bonded bird to learn that he will get enough attention being a good bird; he doesn't have to bite anyone who walks by, or scream, or grab Mom/Dad's favorite knickknack to get attention. Mom/Dad should create many oppor-

Many different stimulating activities are necessary for happy adjustment during the "terrible twos."

tunities to reinforce acceptable independent activities.

This is a particularly significant time for the hyperactive, high-strung hand-fed conures. If they are neglected or isolated at this time of their lives they will most likely learn to bite with great proficiency. I suspect that they do so initially for the enjoyment of the swift reaction from owners. But they eventually get neglected as a result of behavior they originally used to gratify their "excitement" needs, for conures do require stimulating activity. Give them as much exercise as possible as often as possible.

This is also a time when feather chewing may develop, beginning with chewing on the many broken wing and tail feathers that appear as a result of the young bird's clumsiness.

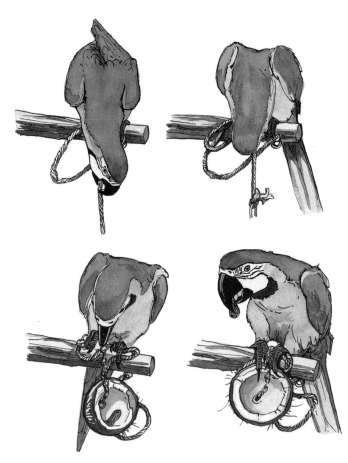

This problem is not unusual in both captive-raised and imported Congo and Timneh African grays and has also been documented by parrot behavior consultant Sally Blanchard. A very short wing trim on a slow-to-molt bird in a dry climate can exacerbate this uncomfortable problem. Keep an eye on broken flight feathers on the wings for early signs of feather chewing and see an avian veterinarian if you suspect that the juvenile parrot is beginning to chew wing feathers. If the problem is severe, the veterinarian might anesthetize the bird and pull the irritating feathers. For some of my clients this operation has seemed like a miracle cure. If left untreated, the bird with damaged wing or tail feathers could progress swiftly or gradually to an all-over feather chewer.

If the bird spends much time alone when human partners are out in the world, be sure that it doesn't have too much unplanned time. A "latchkey" bird who spends the day alone can develop lingering, difficult-to-modify behavior problems, and can be very badly affected during the developmental period. The bird might just sleep all day and expect to be played with all evening, demanding too much attention from an exhausted owner.

In order to develop into a well-adjusted "child," the "toddler" bird must be provided with interaction and stimulation, but that doesn't mean it has to be handled all the time. A parrot is a flocking creature who naturally prefers many side-by-side, doing-things-together activities. Morning human grooming rituals are an excellent time to demonstrate grooming behaviors to your bird and share side-by-side activity.

The chapters to follow give detailed instructions on how to avert behavior problems in the mature companion parrot. Now is the time to establish good habits in a healthy physical and emotional environment for your bird. A skillfully hand-trained young parrot provided with many experiences and lovingly controlled independence will grow into a fine, happy creature. If the step-up command is well reinforced, the trip through the terrible twos can be easily accomplished with merely a wobble correction or two (see page 24); certainly, there will be no human side trip to the hospital for stitches.

Just remember: First, the bird still loves you; it is just testing to see who is "top bird" and who is "bottom bird"; and secondly, *it will pass!*

Chapter 5

Common Behavior Problems

The Importance of Being "Tall"

Height Factors as They Relate to Parrot Disposition

No single environmental factor is more important than the height at which the parrot spends its awake hours. Whether the scenario includes a timid or phobic bird that is housed too low or an aggressive bird that is housed too high, the manipulation of this one element can often produce immediate and stunning changes in the bird.

It is not unusual for a parrot to nip the lower person when it is being passed or handed from a taller person to a shorter person, from an adult to a child, or from a standing person to a sitting person. This does not usually occur because the bird "doesn't like" the shorter person, but because the bird is reinforcing its own perceived dominance over a lower creature.

This nipping-the-shorter-person-when-passed behavior may be easily circumvented by placing the bird on the floor or in a subordinate position where the shorter person will become the taller person. Then, a well-trained person can easily pick the bird up off the floor. That is, if the hand is presented to the "prompt" location on the bird's belly, rather than stuck in the bird's face, the bird will respond appropriately to the prompt by stepping up without a bite.

One of many common calls I receive comes from a man with a young family and a young macaw and goes something like this:

"I purchased my macaw at about the same time my wife had our first child. Alex was a hand-fed baby bird who has been a totally sweet and adorable addition to our family. Our children are three and four now, and the bird is getting more and more aggressive. Alexander is perfect to me, but he has even begun nipping my wife, and I question whether the bird could injure the children."

Because the bird is polite to the man and abuses his loved ones, in the face of *only* this information one might erroneously treat this problem as a matter of jealousy and overbonding to a primary person. This is one more case where observing the environment is necessary to determine whether the behavior stems from juvenile territorialism or from true sexually motivated jealousy.

Usually I go out to the home to find a young bird that is housed in a large commercial parrot cage, perhaps with a permanent or fold-out perch on top of the cage. The bird spends most of its time on the cage or on the man. Most of the bird's "social time"—in the wild this would be foraging time—is spent looking up at the man and down at the woman and children.

If we catch this behavior as it is developing—before it has been reinforced into a habit—and if the bird is not being "baited" by provocative behavior, the problem can usually be eliminated with very simple environmental manipulations and handling adjustments.

I visited a family with a new baby yellow-naped Amazon, a New-World species with remarkable mimicking abilities. It was skinny and poorly feathered, still bearing the broken tail feathers typical of awkward baby birds. The doting family had purchased for their *enfant terrible* a generous cage that placed the bird about six inches higher than any family member. From the top of the cage the creature mutilated any offered hand or digit. At the same time, many of the sounds it made sounded like the whines of a puppy. They were not natural Amazon sounds. The family

couldn't figure out why their bird was whining and attacking them.

Because of the strength and severity of the bites, the father in the family had taken it upon himself to train the bird. His hands were covered with scabs, and he had engaged in several of what the daughter described as "fights" with the bird on top of the cage. The man was highly resistant to the notion of shortening the new cage, which cost over $500. "Shortening" this particular cage involved removing the wheels and a modular section of the tubing that made up the cage "stand." It was a process that required a screwdriver and about 15 minutes.

The problem was solved immediately by forcibly removing the bird from the top of the cage and shortening the cage. Without the false authority afforded by height, this domineering creature was perfectly behaved. From the floor, the bird acted like the family puppy whining to be held. He or she, as the case may be (for most Amazons have no observable gender differences), snuggled into every family member's breast and imitated their shitsu puppy while they cuddled and kissed the creature they thought was vicious.

We removed the stand from under the bird's cage, dropping the height from about 6 feet (2 m) to about 4 feet (1.2 m), and with the use of learned logical aggression-prevention techniques, they have had no further behavior problems. The puppy is grown, but the bird still whines when it wants

In addition to height-related aggression, which may develop if a bird spends all its time in or on a cage like this, a bird confined to a too-small cage with few opportunities for interesting activities may develop unlikable behaviors.

to be held. It has "named" each of the kids with expressions associated with them (It calls the adolescent daughter, "I'm home").

Either the cage must be lowered or the people must be raised. This will instantly, though sometimes only temporarily, terminate the aggressive behavior in a young, well-socialized bird. The new behaviors can then be reinforced with other environmental corrections—such as providing the bird with expanded "foraging" territory, outings with other than the primary person, more baths, and increased or improved exercise.

Another common initial complaint I hear is that a large hookbill "doesn't seem to like its new cage" or that it "has become aggressive since the acquisition of a new cage." Examination of the environment may reveal many sources of this problem, but often the cage is simply too high and the people have lost control of a marginally trained bird.

For reasons both obvious and mysterious, commercial macaw cages seem to wind up housing a macaw in positions dominant over both children and many women. Most commercial parrot cages have at least one place where they may be shortened, either by sawing off some legs, modifying a stand, or by drilling new locations for lower placement of significant parts. In some cases, steps or small "decks" have been constructed to allow the visiting "short ones" to step up as they approach the cage, thereby giving them a place to stand where they are superior to the bird.

Once again, problems related to handling a bird in a higher position can be mitigated by the meticulous training of step-up's. A well-trained hookbill will step onto a long perch presented by a person who is several feet below. This can be very helpful both in the situation described previously and in fly-away situations. The very circumstance of being high is intoxicating to a bird. An impudent little parrot that jumps on the shoulder all the time might bounce around the top of a tree playing "catch me." A well-trained parrot will step up when prompted, even when intoxicated by extreme height. A little tyrant bird will display and threaten when allowed to "hang out" in a high place in the living area; but a well-socialized bird will politely play with toys provided and come down when commanded to do so.

A Bird Needs a Cage

Many common behavior problems in companion parrots may be traced to lack of a suitable cage. The problems are not usually directly caused by lack of a cage. They may be the result of stress compounded by lack of a suitable cage, inappropriate bonding to a person or place due to lack of a cage, lack of exercise, interrupted sleep periods, inappropriate photo periods, harassment by a cage mate, or any one of several other physical and social processes.

Feather chewing, screaming, apathy, aggression, displaced aggression, and sudden nipping are often (but not exclusively) associated with lack of a cage or ill-suited caging. Unacceptable behaviors may develop because of poor adjustment to the color, shape, location, or height of a cage. Failure to provide a cage during the developmental period can lead to many difficult-to-correct problem behaviors.

One of the most common causes of cage-related behavior problems in companion parrots is failure to provide a cage. Surely, a bird needs an open perch or playpen, but a bird also needs a cage.

A room of one's own: Whether a bird is so gregarious it's always into everything or so shy it seeks privacy, a roomy cage out of traffic is needed for good long-term emotional health. A shy bird requires security; a social bird must learn to play alone, thereby preventing the development of dominance behaviors through demands for attention. A bird doing poorly in a shared cage may need to be isolated for protection from abuse by other birds.

A personal gymnasium: A healthy bird is an active bird. Most pet parrots—for reasons of safety and habit—express their energy through climbing, swinging, and flapping.

A bird on a 2-foot long (60 cm) open perch has only 2 *lateral* feet (60 cm) in which to walk back and forth. Adding a 4-foot (1.2 m) rope triples the space to 6 feet (2 m) of climbing and flapping space. A cage only 2 feet square has 4 square feet (.37 m²) on every side and the top—20 *square feet* (1.8 m²) inside and 20 *square feet* (1.8 m²) outside—a total of *40 square feet (3.7 m³) of climbing space!* There is 20 times more climbing surface on a 2 x 2 x 2 foot (60 x 60 x 60 cm) cage than on a 2 foot (60 cm) open perch. Of course, you cannot put a full-sized macaw in a 2 x 2 x 2 foot cage and you can put a macaw on a 2 foot perch. It is a less than ideal situation that should not be considered permanent housing.

A corner to hang out on: Parrots with nonaggressive territorial tendencies may be housed with the cage door open almost all the time. However, at first remove the bird from the cage on your hand in order to maintain social dominance. A well-adjusted bird will spend a good deal of time sitting on the cage on the corner closest to people when there might be a little attention to be had; but it will eat, drink, sleep, and entertain itself inside and outside the cage.

Size: If the cage is the only place the bird has to spend the majority of its time, that cage should be very large indeed, with width and depth and height all being at least 1½ times the bird's extended wingspan. If the cage is smaller than that, the bird should be provided with a foraging or commuting lifestyle.

Configuration: The shape of the cage should include corners. Some birds will be noisy, self-mutilating, phobic, or otherwise ill-at-ease in a round or cylindrical cage. Also, avoid a cage with a solid top. Choose one with a wire top or one composed of bars.

Territory: I do not recommend the cage as the only approved location for a companion parrot to spend time. During most of the year, territorialism, not sexual fugues, appears to be the primary motivation for aggression in medium and larger hookbills. In captivity there appears to be a direct relationship between the amount of space a parrot commands and the intensity with which that territory is defended—the smaller the space, the greater the fervor with which that territory is defended.

Commuting: Unless the cage is the only approved play area, it should be situated well away from human activity areas so that the bird's sleep periods are not interrupted by human activities. A roosting cage might not have much space for silliness, flapping, and climbing. Daily outings to a play area must be provided. This is an excellent opportunity to build a "dependency relationship" with the bird wherein it must rely on its less favorite human companions to provide trans-

A small tree or a large branch mounted in a tub makes an excellent alternative perch or "foraging" territory.

portation daily from the "roost" or sleeping cage to the "foraging area" or playpen.

I believe birds are less likely to become aggressively territorial when they are kept as "commuters" who move frequently from a private roost to a mobile "foraging" area that goes wherever the "flock" goes. A big unpainted basket with the handle wrapped in jute, well-fitted with dishes and toys, and weighted with newspapers is an easy-to-live-with portable foraging area.

Acquisition of a suitable cage and sensitively introducing the bird to the new cage will frequently correct related behavior problems of less than one year's duration. Even a roosting cage that houses the bird at night and infrequently during a part of the day should be at least 1½ times wider than the bird's extended wing span in at least one direction. It should have a tray at least 2 inches (5 cm) deep. Food and water dishes should be ac-

cessible to servicing from outside the cage; and if the bird likes to tear up stuff in the bottom of the cage, there should be a grill at least an inch or two (2.5–5 cm) above the tray.

Introducing a new cage: Although many birds exhibit immediate and delighted response to a new cage, some birds must be enticed to accept a new cage. In the face of reluctance, place the cage in the bird's favorite place and set the old cage on the floor lower than the new cage with a branch or ladder between them. After a day or so, remove food and water dishes, then a day or two later remove the perches from the old cage. Place food and water dishes on top of the new cage, then gradually move them inside the cage. An older bird that has been in the same cage for many years —even if it is a small inadequate

cage—may have strong emotional ties that must be broken gradually over a period of time. The object of the new cage is to reduce stress, not cause it, so give the bird at least a couple of days before removing that old cage.

Because parrots will play with any element of their environment, provide them with food and water dishes that cannot be moved.

The Screaming Parrot

As previously discussed, the parrot is a verbal creature, "prompting" parents to provide food and care by vocalizing even from within the egg. The parrot is also a very social creature. These two natural tendencies combine to create the ability and desire to learn human speech. They are also responsible for the development of screaming behaviors.

Some loud vocalization is part of a parrot's natural expression such as: "Wake up, it's morning!," "Everybody go to roost, it's getting dark!," "Here I am, I'm a cockatoo!," and "Sing along with me."

When evaluating a "screaming problem," begin with a diary to document the times, duration, and intensity of screaming. Some types of parrots have a greater tendency to scream, and some types have natural calls or "voices" that humans find annoying. It is probably easier for a person to endure twenty minutes of blue crown conure screaming than ten minutes of Moluccan cockatoo screaming or even five minutes of Patagonian conure screaming. Usually, more than three to five minutes of screaming at a time more than five times a day (except for "singing" along with music or stimulating sounds like the shower) is unnatural for most species and problematic in human living situations.

Screaming is a learned behavior. It can be picked up from other birds, crying babies or barking dogs. A parrot can teach itself to scream. This behavior is easily (usually unintentionally) reinforced by humans. Ignoring the behavior increases the calling response. Punishments increase frustration levels and often exacerbate screaming. Screaming is best controlled with anticipation and prevention.

Hunger or thirst: Empty cups can easily contribute to the development of a screaming problem. Birds normally scream at feeding time. In the wild, loud calls accompany their arrival at foraging areas, inviting the flock to dine. A companion bird knows when it's time to eat; and if food or water isn't there, Paco will scream, "Where's dinner?"

Isolation: A bird that is isolated from flock, family, or mate will call out for its buddies. Visual isolation as well as actual physical isolation can stimulate speech and/or screaming. Talking or soft whistling back and forth with the bird will model the desired response. A screaming bird can sometimes be placated with the addition of well situated mirrors so that human companions are visible around that kitchen or living room corner.

Boredom: Parrots are extremely intelligent. In addition to toys of *their* choice, they need visual stimulation. Sight is their most highly developed sense, and television is the easiest way to entertain a lonely parrot. A bird sitting at home all day is resting up for play time. Just when Mom or Dad needs rest, Paco is ready for fun and games. A television on a timer set to come on a few hours before the humans get home will use some of that pent-up bird energy. Never forget or underestimate a parrot's love of squealing and flashing lights and bells.

Eating and the related "foraging" (digging through the bowl, tonguing things) are excellent distractions from screaming related to boredom. Withhold food from the bird for a few hours, then place an interesting and diverse assortment of food in the bowl just *before* the bird would usually begin to scream.

Lack of exercise: A healthy parrot has lots of energy. If there is no provision for flapping, screaming or feather chewing can take its place. To encourage flapping, provide climbing and swinging toys; or place the wing-trimmed bird on the hand then move the hand down quickly so that the bird flaps its wings; or swing the bird on a knotted rope (sensitively, of course) until it is breathing heavier. A sedentary parrot beginning an exercise program may become winded in only a few seconds, but exercise time can be gradually increased. If the bird is mature and has had neither exercise nor a vet check for some time, a visit to an avian veterinarian should be made before beginning an exercise program for the control of screaming.

Bathing is a logical follow-up to aerobics. A fine-mist shower sprayed from below to fall down on the bird is a fitting reward for exercise. Many parrots will continue flapping and having "silly attacks" during a spray bath.*

A bird that is busy "zipping" wet feathers (preening) after a bath is not screaming.

Desire for a mate: A bird with out-of-control hormones may call incessantly for a nonexistent mate. Some of this may be seasonal; some may be modified with diet. Breeders have long understood that birds can be stimulated to breed with the addition of animal protein, specifically eggs, to the diet. I believe I see increased aggression and screaming in companion parrots with diets including more than 18 percent animal protein, particularly if the primary source of that protein is eggs. If you don't want your bird to exhibit breeding behavior, avoiding feeding eggs. Try substituting cheese, tofu, or tuna for daily protein.

There are *many* other reasons for screaming and many other techniques to modify screaming. Some causes are easy to figure out; some are very subtle. An avian behavior consultant may be able to tell to what extent screaming can be modified in a particular bird by evaluating the home environment, taking a detailed history, manipulating and reevaluating the environment. Don't give up! It might take more than one try, but the peace is well worthwhile!

*I believe it is dangerous and confusing to spray a stream of water as a punishment. Bathing should be a welcome reward. A bird that is punished with water can develop other neurotic behaviors such as feather chewing and foul temper.

A Bird's Gotta Chew What a Bird's Gotta Chew

Particularly in the time of year perceived by companion birds to be "springtime," our feathered friends use their beaks to reduce everything they can reach to toothpicks (in the case of small parrots, confetti). Along with annual screaming and hormonal rites, parrots are eagerly expressing their sexuality by demonstrating their cavity-building (demolition) skills.

I am often asked to correct chewing behaviors. These are some of my favorite calls, for the remedy, though ever so tricky, is easily accessible to *most* parrot owners.

Anticipation: Just as a caring owner knows the dog needs a bone, a parrot owner knows the bird needs something to chew. A busy bird is a happy bird, and chewing is a major form of parrot entertainment. Controlling destructive chewing is accomplished by anticipating the bird's needs and providing appropriate chewables. Lovebirds, cockatiels, and budgies like the cardboard rolls from inside toilet paper. Larger hookbills like clean wood scraps (*not pressure treated*) from the home workshop.

A variety of textures and densities are desirable, but wooden toys of medium hardness encourage just the right amount of chewing instinct. Very soft wood chewables too readily stimulate the bird's reproductive instincts,

and very hard chewables eventually prove boring (although one or two hard wood toys will prevent your having to replace all toys weekly).

While wood, and hard nuts, including coconut are favored, resilient (not brittle) plastic and very strong Plexiglas are also fun for an enterprising hookbill. Chains of plastic shower curtain rings will stand up to some birds, but the more costly toys in the pet store are worth more because they are made to safely withstand those relentless beaks.

Kaku, a lesser sulphur, can destroy a set of shower curtain rings in a day, but those heavy plastic chains from

Be sure the bird is merely destroying the toy, not swallowing it. If there is any question about whether a bird is ingesting chewed-off portions of an inorganic toy, the toy should be allowed only with supervision. Design the environment to ensure that chewed up bits of wood, cardboard, or leather wind up on the floor rather than in the water bowl.

Controlled accessibility: If someone reports that their bird is chewing up the picture frame, lamp shade, chair, banister, or baskets, it's obvious that the bird is very much loved, or it wouldn't have access to the picture frame, chair, baskets, and the like. But respecting each other's space and property is an important part of a successful long-term relationship, and a relationship with a parrot has the potential to span generations.

You deserve to have your things respected by the bird just as surely as the bird has a right to its own space and things. That is not to say that the bird should be isolated. An isolated bird will develop screaming behaviors, become self-mutilating, or will emotionally withdraw into a zombielike state. The bird must be trained to stay in a "parrot-proofed" area not unlike a toddler's playpen. A bird with trimmed wing feathers that has not been allowed to roam is easily trained to stay in an open play area.

Put the bird on a stimulating playpen designed without easy accessibility to the floor. Provide plenty of toys and entertainment. If the bird

the pet store keep her busy for a week or so. It is particularly important to keep Kaku entertained, because if she's bored (like many of her kind) she chews her own feathers. It's not a pretty hobby! Destructible toys help prevent the onset of feather chewing for most birds. In the case of a bird that can destroy a toy in minutes, indestructible toys supplemented with destructible toys are necessary to control the boredom that sets in when the toy is "finished."

leaves the play area, lock it in its cage for a short time. Use a stern termination stimulus such as *"Get in Jail!"* (The sharp "t" sound is important.) Be sure there is as much food, water, and stimulation on the play area as there is in the cage, lest the bird start "acting out" to get to the cage.

A "dual area" play space—perhaps two perches side by side or a hanging playpen linked to a floor perch by a knotted rope, or two hanging baskets connected with a rope—is sometimes helpful in training the bird to stay put. This works by providing the bird an acceptable choice of location.

When training the bird to stay on the playpen, be watchful. If it looks as if the bird is going to try to roam, clap your hands loudly and say *"Don't! You'll Get in Jail!"* This warning with familiar words should stimulate the bird to terminate the undesirable behavior. The verbal warning may be reinforced with your display of displaced aggression, such as a clap of the hands or a little aerobic exercise. This also reinforces the dominance hierarchy—that you are the boss. Hand the bird a toy or treat to take its mind off roaming. With a very few repetitions properly administered, most individual birds will figure out that they must stay in the play area unless invited elsewhere.*

*Among the most difficult-to-contain roamers and chewers are the small cockatoos (Goffin's, bare-eyes, lessers, rosies) and the full-sized macaws. They are also often escape artists. I can't tell you how many parrots I've met named Houdini!

Distraction: It is extremely important for that beak to have something to chew on *all the time*. It is sometimes helpful to withhold some special chewable or keep some favorites in reserve as a distraction for that special time when the obsession to explore and chew is strongest.

Actual physical punishment does not work usually with birds; it merely frightens, injures, or enrages them and does nothing to modify their behavior. Some people punish almost any "misbehavior" in a pet parrot with sensory deprivation: covering or isolation. In the case of chewing, which is, of course, *not* a misbehavior, I believe anticipation, controlled accessibility, and distraction are not only more humane, but ultimately more effective. Reward a quiet, busy parrot enjoying its own space with words, petting, food treats, or toys. A properly trained or contained bird provided with lots of options and an ever-evolving supply of varied approved chewables will have no opportunity or

Rose-breasted cockatoos (left) and Goffin's cockatoos (right) are rarely willing to stay on their approved perches.

need to eat grandma's 150-year-old clock or the new entertainment center.

Exercise and the Companion Parrot

When a companion parrot is denied appropriate exercise both its health and behavior are affected. A healthy parrot has an enormous amount of energy. As in humans, if that energy is not expressed through physical activity, it must come out somehow. Adequate physical activity can reduce or eliminate behaviors such as screaming, biting, feather chewing, failure to bathe, failure to groom, excessive demands for attention, and compulsive masturbation, not to mention obesity and related poor cardiovascular condition in tame companion birds.

Flapping is the exercise of choice for the most effective use of bird energy. Exercise might or might not include the human partner. A well-adjusted avian companion provided with enough space and equipment will usually, but not always, learn to exercise on its own. "Enough space" is room to spread and flap wings without hitting them on anything. Proper equipment includes swings, large branches extending over the cage, and toys hanging above the cage on which the bird can climb and flap.

While a sedentary bird that has been sitting and cuddling for a long time might, at first, resist exercise, the long-term benefits make a *gradually* increasing program well worth the effort. One particularly beneficial use of human-generated exercise is in the modification of screaming. If the bird screams when the owner leaves the room, the owner returns immediately to the room as if responding to the call, picks up and greets the bird, then gives the bird the above-described aerobic exercise. The bird is first con-

The Benefits of Exercise

A bird following an exercise program may exhibit unexpected benefits. A few years ago I visited a client who complained that his 2½-year-old greenwing macaw "danced" constantly when he was in the room. Although the bird was not screaming, the incessant hyperactivity was maddening to the owner. I suggested responding to the behavior with "aerobics": placing the bird on the hand, moving the hand down with just enough speed to require the bird to flap its wings until it was slightly winded. At first, the bird was able to do aerobics for about 15 seconds at a time. Within a few weeks it was up to 40 seconds. Within a few months, the first three primary flight feathers, which had been damaged since the bird was a baby, were showing signs of regrowth. The end feathers on one wing had been pronounced permanently "lost" by two eminently qualified avian veterinarians; but apparently, improved circulation to the wings stimulated the follicles, after two years, to regrow feathers. The owner was happy to report that the bird discontinued the demanding behavior and learned to play alone.

ditioned to the exercise in a friendly, sensitive way, so that it will know there is no threat involved; but eventually, this response can take on the tone of "do 20" (as in sit-ups or laps around the gym).

A demanding bird quickly learns that screaming when its owner leaves the room brings a gym teacher who *requires* a beneficial activity that is not what the bird wanted at that time. Even if you have to remove the bird from the cage, required exercise often works immediately to inspire the bird to discontinue the demanding behavior. It should be preceded by a threat, or displaced aggression, or a termination stimulus—a stern look or strong words like "Cut it out!"—that warn of impending undesirable consequences so that future infractions can be avoided without disciplinary action.

Unfortunately, forced flapping works best for macaws and pudgy Amazons and not active little conures who may come to view aerobics as a new fun game. Aerobics might actually excite some birds, exasperating the problem behavior. This activity is to be done sensitively, of course, as some birds actually hate it, and may withdraw, temporarily, from the administering party. It may be an effective deterrent in the case of an overbonded bird who is so crazy about one individual that it attacks others.

Other easy ways to inspire avian exercise:

- Provide a knotted, free-swinging rope or ring and bell toy for the bird to climb. The rings should be large enough to allow the bird's whole body to pass through or too small for the bird to insert its head.
- Play hide-and-seek and peep-eye around corners in unfamiliar territory; try to make the bird chase you to avoid being left alone in a strange place. It's not a good idea to encourage a bird, particularly a hand-fed bird, to roam around unsupervised.
- Play with the bird with a knotted rope, gently swinging the bird as it holds the rope with beak or claws (do this in an open area, so if the bird lets go it won't smash into something).
- Make the bird seek you out —including climbing up your body without assistance—if it wants to get off the floor.

- Parrot behavior consultant Sally Blanchard suggests playing "fetch" as you would with a dog. Entice the bird to return with the small bauble by saying "Good bird." Reward a successful fetch with further praise and petting.
- Sensitively throw the feather-trimmed bird onto the bed or sofa or to its cage so that it "flies" the last few feet.
- It is important that a parrot have a cage for numerous climbing opportunities rather than just a perch. (A perch is approximately 2 linear feet (60 cm) whereas a 2 foot x 2 foot x 2 foot (60 cm x 60 cm x 60 cm) cage is 40 square feet ($3.7m^2$) or 20 times more climbing space)
- Provide a "climbing tree" or large natural branch. Put rings or grapes on the ends of all the twigs so that the bird has to climb around to eat or remove them.

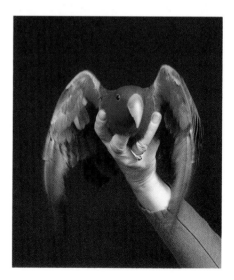

Exercise is a simple cure for many parrot behavior problems. A bird that is just sitting around all day will improvise behaviors such as screaming and nipping, or might commence nesting behaviors such as sitting in the corner and chewing or laying eggs. Encouraging exercise can return a truculent teenager or mature bird back into the sweetly disposed animal we remember.

Toys!

Toys are absolutely necessary for good physical, emotional, and behavioral adjustment in a captive parrot. Avian expert and biologist Dr. Matthew Vriends reports that foraging for food consumes more than 90 percent of the wild parrot's daily activity. Try as we might, we can't replicate all elements of a wild environment. In captivity, providing food eliminates the need to forage, creating a need for other activities, and therefore toys.

Toys provide opportunities for decision making, intellectual development, physical exercise, the release of aggression, nurturing instincts, and other role-playing behaviors. From a feather or a sliver of wood used to scratch to a spoon for eating, birds love to use simple tools, and toys are simply tools for fun. A parrot that is not provided with toys will improvise makeshift toys out of its own feathers, slivers or chips of wood, food, cage parts, dishes, or any other environmental elements it can reach.

A wise owner provides lots of safe-for-the-bird toys so that the bird does not injure itself or the environment by creating toys such as electrical cords, plants, furniture, walls, or other objects that have not been safety-tested for birds.

The activity provided by toys is essential for long life and good health. Avian interactions with toys also provide hours of happy entertainment for humans. A bird who has learned to play alone is a treasured companion indeed.

Electrical cords are not toys!

Stimulation provided by toys is particularly important during the developmental period called the "terrible twos." Toys reinforce good social development by providing opportunities for role playing, successful decision making, and distraction from socially unacceptable habits. Many birds "parent" their toys in much the same way as their owners "parent" them, scolding and punishing as well as soothing, feeding, and rewarding.

Quite a few commercial parrot toys are designed to simulate parenting roles. The Polly Dolly is a parent-role toy consisting of cloth, string, leather, jute, wood, and a bell. It is an excellent stimulus for nurturing and "preening." This toy is an extremely beneficial distraction for feather chewers. Watch out for a bird with no other behavioral problems becoming overly attached, and therefore aggressive around the toy.

A young parrot in the developmental period should be given at least two new toys at a time. A mature companion parrot should have a minimum of one new indestructible or semi-destructible toy monthly. A healthy parrot requires many destructible toys monthly, and if they are not provided, they will be "found."

The cardboard rolls from inside paper towels and toilet paper are excellent chewables, as are clean, nontoxic bottle caps; but avoid excessive colored ink, staples, carbon and carbonless paper. The cardboard rolls may be cut into large cardboard "beads" and strung on rope or twine.

It's surprising how very often a parrot behavior consultant, when confronted with a two- or three-year-old bird who is biting out of control, hears the following story:

"Well, we gave him a toy once, when we first got him; but he didn't play with it, so we didn't give him another one."

With an examination of the bird's environment and a little prodding, the owners might remember that the bird responds to the telephone and the doorbell, opens the cage door, opens the food-service doors, swings on the door, bangs the carrying handle around on top of the cage, and makes soup in his water bowl with anything he can find. It is easy to figure out how the bird entertained itself. It had lots of toys; it just didn't have planned toys, commercially designed toys, or socially productive toys.

These cardboard rolls can be punctured in numerous places and have short lengths of jute, twine, or shoelaces pulled through the holes and knotted. A nut or a few sunflower seeds might be placed inside a cardboard roll which could then be closed at the ends with biodegradable tape. Punch a few holes in the cardboard so that the bird can see what's moving around inside, and Paco will spend much happy time removing the contents from inside the roll. Any of these paper products may contain toxic inks or glues, so watch to see if they wind up in the water bowl and eliminate them if the bird insists on soaking paper or cardboard remnants.

Cages are the gymnasium of the companion parrot and climbing toys are their exercise equipment. Most parrot-type birds have an innate love of swinging and should be offered at least one swing in their environment. Other favored climbing toys include knotted natural ropes, ladders, branches, chains, or anything hanging from a chain. When suspending hanging toys from the ceiling, it is advisable to provide some form of protection for the ceiling, perhaps a pizza pan with a hole drilled in the middle with the ceiling hook passing through the hole in the pizza pan.

I believe every physically and emotionally healthy parrot-type bird needs at least one hanging toy. When asked to identify the best all-around bird toy, I unhesitatingly recommend a contraption sometimes marketed under the name "Olympic Rings." It is a series of hanging, interlocking rings with a bell connected to the bottom.

The rings should be large enough

to allow the bird to pass completely through them. They should be hung in or over the cage in a space large enough to allow the bird to hang on to the toy and flap. As the bird climbs in and around higher rings, the bell and the lower ring will jingle enticingly. Your bird will enjoy a lifetime of fun and physical exercise with this mini-gymnasium, and it will do so *without you*!

This particular toy comes in metal and bamboo versions. The bamboo version is inexpensive and perfect for cockatiels, parakeets, lovebirds, lories, and other small hookbills. It will, of course, be destroyed periodically. The metal version of this toy is virtually indestructible. The bell must be replaced periodically, of course, as enterprising parrots feel obliged to remove the clapper. There are cockatiel/conure-sized versions of this toy as well as Amazon-sized Olympic Rings readily available in metal, but these are not quite large enough for a full-sized cockatoo or macaw. A wrought iron company or individual who makes security bars can custom make this very important piece of equipment in sizes large enough and sturdy enough to accommodate the large hookbills.

Since most conscientious parrot owners keep their bird's wing feathers trimmed for safety purposes, this toy is a fun way for the bird to achieve the exercise necessary to keep physically fit. It will help to prevent the onset of noise and behavior problems in large and small parrots.

Watch out for hanging toys with rings that are large enough for the bird's head, but too small to allow the bird to withdraw the head easily.

Many birds also enjoy holding toys. One of the favorite toys of many large cockatoos is a metal spoon. Not only do these birds often learn to eat and drink with their spoon, but they just love to watch humans jump when they drop the spoon, making a loud noise.

Toys may be used for overt behavioral purposes. Holding toys are an excellent "distraction device" for birds with a fascination for buttons, jewelry, and eyeglasses. If the bird goes for bright items, look for a brightly colored holding toy. If the bird will play only with destructible holding toys, get destructible holding toys. Little wooden barbells, the fruit-juice colored wooden lollipops, and regular Tinkertoys are good for this. Greg Harrison and Chris Davis in their chapter on behavior modification in

Clinical Avian Medicine and Surgery suggest that a favorite toy withheld during the day may help to distract a parrot from after-work screaming.

Many parrots are particularly fascinated with toys that have moving parts or make noise. The new lines of Plexiglas toys with moving parts are exceptionally beautiful and durable. Kitchen measuring spoons that are linked together (metal or plastic) or old keys are suitable occasional or emergency toys (with supervision only), but these may present a hazard if the bird has a tendency to pry open the metal rings that attach them.

Puzzle Toys must be taken apart to reach a reward such as a nut. Parrots love those wooden cages with peanuts inside. Most types of parrots merely chew the bars away to get to the peanuts. Occasionally, we hear of a lory or quaker who manipulates the peanuts out of the cage without chewing through the bars.

Food Toys, including whole, hard nuts such as walnuts or Brazil nuts are interesting and nourishing. Several lines of toys now incorporate nuts into their design. Interesting toys may be fabricated from coconuts, which are highly caloric and helpful in putting weight on a stubborn eater. Avoid pits such as cherry, peach, or avocado; they look as if they might be fun to play with, but several of them are toxic.

Interactive Toys: There are now available, waterproof electronic bird-activated music boxes. I believe we are just a few years away from bird-activated interactive speech training devices.

A parrot that has received no new environmental stimulation in quite some time may be reluctant to play with new toys. Inducing a parrot-type bird to play with toys can almost always be accomplished by stuffing the toys with paper towels or by tying knots of paper towels to the toys (leave the corners of the paper towels sticking out). Real paper towels or unprinted newsprint are the papers of choice for inducing chewing and playing.

Care should be taken to ensure that the parrot is not ingesting pieces of toys or soaking them in the water bowl. Breakable and chewable inorganic (plastic, nylon, etc.) toys should be provided only with supervision. Toys provided without human supervision should be unbreakable (metal or Plexiglas, etc.). In particular, watch out for bells with lead clappers

Difficult-to-access foods, such as this crab's leg, can provide hours of amusement (and some nourishment).

and holding or sitting-on-the-floor toys with lead weights. No toy should be considered 100 percent safe. A really creative bird can make a hazard out of almost any toy.

A well-adjusted hookbill with a new toy is quite a sight. I always wonder what it thinks it is doing. The bird will grab the new toy and feverishly begin "working" it. You can almost see the little brain wheels turning. "I've got to get this thing apart *right now*!"

Grooming to Save a Parrot's Life

Just as failure to contain a dog or cat is the greatest cause of injury, loss, and death, failure to properly trim wing feathers is probably the greatest cause of injury, loss, and death to uncaged companion birds. But containment isn't the only reason to groom a bird. The periodic mainte-

nance of wings, toenails, and beak is necessary for safe, successful living-room lifestyles.

Unfortunately, new bird owners sometimes mistakenly believe that wing clipping is an "inhumane" solution to dangers inside and outside the home. Probably the reverse is true. This simple, nonsurgical procedure resembles a haircut and must be repeated with similar frequency.

Some of the most heartbreaking injuries seen by avian veterinarians—fried, boiled, or outright burned pet birds—are the direct result of allowing free flight in the home. Death caused by startled birds flying into uncovered expanses of glass, mirror, or ceiling fans are totally preventable with periodic wing trims. Drowning—possibly the most frequent cause of death in the home—is prevented with wing trims combined with toilet bowl covering and the practice of not leaving sinks, tubs, pots, glasses, or containers of water or other liquids uncovered in the presence of unsupervised companion birds.

I believe companion animals are benefited by their association with humans. A domestic cat living wild has a life expectancy of less than a year. An Amazon parrot which has a life expectancy of less than 10 years in the wild may live well past 50 in captivity. Appropriate and reasonable care favorably alter the companion animal's life expectancy. Timely wing feather trims are a big part of appropriate and reasonable care.

Since wing feathers do not grow continuously, they may be compared to human eyebrows. Growing to a certain length, they remain that length until they fall out and are replaced. Feathers remain the trimmed length until they fall out and are replaced by whole feathers. Timely regular clipping will not completely prevent a bird from flying. Wing trimming will, optimally, prevent boisterous flying in the house—like preventing children from running on a wet swimming pool sidewalk. A well-clipped pet bird retains balance and self-confidence while forfeiting the ability to gain altitude.

The "utility clip" is probably the most dependable, widely-accepted clipping configuration. It involves the clipping of the first eight or nine primary flight feathers (ten long feathers on the ends of the wing that slant away from the body) just at the point where they are covered by the next layer of feathers.

A very light-bodied bird (cockatoo, cockatiel, parakeet, or dove) may require the trimming of all ten primaries and, perhaps, even a couple of the secondary flight feathers (ten lower inside wing feathers that slant toward the body) to restrict altitude.

Another popular clip is the "modified show" clip or "escape artist" clip, which leaves the two longest primary feathers and trims back the other eight flight feathers from there. This may be successfully employed only with heavy bodied birds like African grays, *some* Amazons, and some macaws. It is not recommended by most professional groomers who might be held liable if a treasured companion bird flew away.

Joe Southern, who operates Colorado's largest bird grooming business says, "You can trim literally every feather except the longest primary flights on a cockatiel, and many of them can still fly very well. I am often called to reclip birds trimmed in this fashion. Many of these, as well as birds with only one wing clipped, can fly better than their new owners thought a full-flighted bird could."

The "escape artist" clip leaves those two long end feathers vulnerable to being caught in cage bars or knocked out. Birds regain flight capacity more quickly, sometimes when only one or two feathers regrow. This clip must be meticulously maintained—trimming new feathers as soon as they no longer have the retained sheath indicating blood supply. This clip is not at all dependable for a

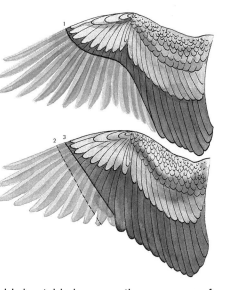

Top: An appropriate wing trim for light-bodied birds, such as cockatoos, cockatiels, and conures. Bottom: Less severe trims for heavy-bodied birds, such as African grays and Amazons. The least severe cut is for clumsy baby African grays who fall frequently.

bird outside because the presence of wind and enough space to catch the wind is all that is needed for flight.

Visually check a bird perched on the hand by holding the foot and moving the hand down with just enough speed to require the spreading of wings. Clip regrowth as it appears. A functional test of flight ability may be made in a carpeted area by standing across the room from the cage and gently lofting the bird toward the cage. A flighted bird will usually elect to fly to the cage. A properly clipped bird will flutter down to the floor.

Neither visual checks nor functional indoor tests can truly demonstrate that a bird cannot gain altitude. Outdoor excursions are always risky. A bird that is too lazy to fly across the room might be frightened enough to fly into a dog run or busy street in an uncontrolled outdoor setting. It can be a heartbreaking experience.

The regular trimming of wing feathers no more inhibits a parrot's "true nature" than spaying or neutering a cat inhibits its "true nature." A spayed female cat never misses the "joys" of kittens and motherhood. In the presence of other appropriate care, a parrot who has never "prowled" the dangerous neighborhood skies proceeds in normal, birdlike fashion to have a full and joyous life.

Untrimmed toenails can also be life threatening to a companion parrot. Because of the physical structure of the parrot's feet—with four toes, two opposing two—a parrot climbing on a wire cage must be able to stretch the foot completely open to "unhook" toenails from the pair of cage bars usually spanned by the foot. If the toenails become too long, the bird may not be able to open the foot wide enough to climb easily from place to place in the cage. If the bird is frightened it might merely break a leg; if it panics and cannot get loose from the bars, it might die. If it does not die from the stress of being caught on the cage bars, it might die of thirst because it cannot reach the water supply.

Sharp toenails are necessary in the wild where a fallen bird might be dinner; but in a companion parrot, they can negatively affect the human/ avian relationship by causing pain to the handling humans. Unintentional reactions by humans to sharp toenails may cause biting by the bird, changing loyalties by the bird, or insecurity on the part of both humans and bird. The owner of a poorly groomed and poorly trained parrot may go to work on Monday looking like a weekend intravenous drug user or a victim of spouse abuse.

Most parrots must be restrained for nail grooming, but some parrots, particularly hand-fed parrots, initiated early to nail clipping as a part of social interaction, learn to allow nail grooming without restraint. This makes the whole process more enjoyable for both humans and bird. But one of the most obvious behavioral advantages of grooming is that the parrot becomes used to the restraint. Not only is the occasionally restrained bird more cooperative overall (just as frequently groomed dogs are said to have better dispositions), the frequently groomed bird who is accustomed to restraint fares better during veterinary care when restraint stress might mean the difference between life and death. A thorough behavioral evaluation usually includes a description of "grooming stress" or lack thereof. Frequent grooming by the same handler reduces or almost totally eliminates grooming stress in most well adjusted birds.

I see less towel fear with a towel that is approximately the color of the bird; but any neutral, solid color towel that is free of strings or loose threads will suffice as an appropriate restraint garment. Approach from the front, below the bird, holding one end of the towel in each hand with the middle of the towel drooping around the bird's breast. Completely, loosely envelop the bird in the towel, moving your less-dominant hand to the back of the bird's neck. Holding through the towel, grip the bird around the neck with the thumb and forefinger touching, or in the case of a very large bird almost touching just below the bird's beak. Position the bird so that the towel may be opened from the front. Check to see that there is no pressure from the hand or towel on the bird's eyes. Check to see that the bird's breast is not restrained. Because a parrot has no diaphragm, the chest must move in and out to draw air into the lungs and air sacs.

With the help of an assistant, you can either ball the foot and expose the toe and nail on the opposing side of the foot or gently pull the two opposing toes on one foot apart and clip the tip from the nail. Be careful to avoid the vein that supplies blood to the nail. In light-colored nails this can be seen easily with back light. It is more difficult with dark toenails. Bleeding is always a possibility. A dependable coagulant such as Kwik-Stop or silver nitrate should be readily available in the event of a bleeding toenail.

In an emergency one might cauterize the nail with a hot, recently blown-out match or a heated fork tine. Many professional groomers use a grinding tool such as a Dremel to reduce sharp toenails on medium and larger hook-bills. While it is slightly more time consuming than clipping the nails, there is usually no danger of bleeding. In addition, the ground toenail is immediately smooth and comfortable for the human hand. There is also a grooming tool which uses heat to melt or burn the nail back.

I believe most companion parrot relationships are best served by having a professional groomer, an outsider, perform regular maintenance on wing feathers, toenails, and beaks. This protects the sensitive, trusting relationship you have worked so hard to build.

Sometimes, however, with the more aggressive species such as Amazons and macaws, certain advantages accrue from having the best-loved human perform the grooming chores. If the bird is over-bonded to a particular person either of two behaviorally desirable things might happen.

One, the bird might withdraw a little from the person to whom it is over-bonded and cease attacking other household humans.

Or, two, the bird might decide it actually enjoys the grooming process, which could in itself strengthen the human/bird bond. I have seen quite a few conures and brotogeris who loved to have the tip gently filed off the upper mandible with an emery board. This is the only nonprofessional form of beak grooming I advocate, for the stress involved in grinding a bird's beak can kill the bird. Most beak grooming should be done only by professionals. In particular, infrequently groomed birds (less than once a year) or birds in poor health should be groomed only by an experienced avian veterinarian. Watch the bird's response during grooming. Unless you

are very faint of heart, don't let someone groom the bird outside your presence. If the bird hates the groomer or the groomer seems to handle the bird poorly, look for another groomer.

Grooming is more important to parrots than to any other companion animal. Whether from a frying pan accident, an accidental fly-away, or a caught toenail, an ungroomed bird faces a life filled with danger and the potential for tragic and untimely death.

Birds and Bathing

Bathing is an extremely pleasurable activity for birds. With the exception of the African grays, both Congo and Timneh, most common companion parrots take to it like the proverbial duck. Accompanied by comical postures and silly sounds, a spray

bath may be the very first way a new owner/bird team can entertain friends and family.

Small parrots bathe readily in water dishes. Some parrots, like lories, literally bathe their water away several times a day and must be monitored frequently to guard against a dry water bowl (it is also helpful to provide a water tube for drinking). Gray-cheeked parakeets have even been known to cause their own screaming problems by bathing away their water, and then screaming their little blue heads off because there is nothing to drink. (In the presence of a screaming problem, check first to see if there is food and water). Mid-sized and larger hookbills seem to prefer a fine spray mist bath, which should be provided (except in extremely cold weather) a couple of times a week.

When introducing a new or reluctant parrot to spray baths, begin with a clean, new bottle filled with fresh tap water that has not been allowed to stand and grow dangerous micro-organisms. Watch out for very hard water, overtreated water, or water suspected of harboring giardia. This little parasite is not unusual in mountain communities, particularly during spring runoff. It is a common cause of illness-related feather chewing and can kill both chicks and adult birds.

As with the introduction of new foods, a parrot may be reluctant to enjoy this new activity, but planning and persistence pay off. A hot sunny afternoon is ideal, as the bird will naturally wish to cool off. If the bird has never been sprayed, it is sometimes helpful to run the dishwasher, vacuum cleaner, hair dryer or shower, as these sounds will help stimulate the bird's desire to bathe. Set the nozzle for the finest possible mist, hold the bottle at least a foot away from the bird, lower than the bird, and spray a continuous mist above the bird's head so that water falls down on the bird like rain in the forest. It is sometimes helpful to make soothing, cooing noises when initiating a bird to the spray mist bath. Amazons, cockatoos, and macaws may scream with delight and enjoy having accompaniment (you!) in their screaming.

An effectively bathed bird will look a little like a drowned rat. This may be difficult to accomplish on a healthy, dusty cockatoo who has not been bathed recently. Even a bird whose feathers are not repelling the water

Although structurally perfect, some of this bird's feathers look bad because they are not clean.

Parrots are more likely to respond favorably to a spray bath if the spray bottle is held lower than the bird and the water falls down like rain from over the bird's head.

will require at least a couple of quarts of water for a good bath. If it is cold outside, be sure the room is at least 70–75°F (21–23.8°C). If tap water is extremely cold, the air will further cool it, so start with warm, almost hot water. When it is cold outside, it may be best to bathe the bird in a warm bathroom, then blow dry with a hair dryer or direct a heat lamp toward the bird until it is *absolutely dry*. Many birds will respond to the hair dryer with exactly the same delight as the spray bath.

Because bathing is a community ritual for these flocking birds, behavioral benefits accrue from the sharing of a shower by bird and owner. I believe a new bird should first observe the owner sleeping (also a shared flock activity) and then see the owner eat and bathe to establish common (behavioral) ground upon which to build a relationship. Many caring owners include their parrots in their own daily grooming rituals, beginning with a shower. Provide a comfortable perch such as a wooden 2 x 2 on top of the shower door or perhaps a wooden dowel for the shower curtain. There are several manufactured shower perches available. While some birds actually like the water as it comes directly from the shower head, I believe it is usually too strong and can drown the poor bird. An active shower with strong water pressure will deflect water off the human body onto the bird; but the spray bottle remains the safest, most effective way to include a parrot in human bathing rituals. Ideally, there will be much singing of duets.

If the owner bathes rather than showers, the spray bottle will be a necessary accessory for the bird's benefit. Then, of course, the bird must not be left unsupervised with a bathtub full of water or an uncovered toilet.

Showering with the bird by the less-than-favorite owner is an excellent way to work on the modification of overbonding. Even if you can't usually handle the bird, take the bird on a

A bird enjoying a bath will get sillier as it gets wetter. It may exhibit the same or an even more enthusiastic response to being blown dry with a hair dryer.

perch to the bathroom, share a shower and a song, and watch the relationship improve!

Letting the bird observe and groom during human grooming rituals—shaving, blowing hair dry, etc.—will further reinforce the "flock-likeness" of the parrot and its people. Aerosols such as deodorant and hair spray should be applied only after the bird has been removed from the area.

In addition to numerous behavioral advantages, bathing provides health benefits. Infrequently bathed birds have ratty-looking, sometimes tattered feathers. They may become feather chewers as a result of trying to groom dirty or brittle feathers. Bathing promotes tight, well-locked feathers and supple feather condition. In dry climates, infrequent spraying (along with a vitamin A deficiency) may contribute to the development of allergies, disease, or sinus problems.

Bathing is one of the easiest ways to improve the behavior of even poorly socialized birds. It is a basic avian need. Without the healthful recreational diversion of frequent drenching showers, a companion parrot may become a screamer, biter, or feather chewer; but probably Paco will merely be cranky and dirty.

Behavioral Feather Chewing

As a veteran fingernail biter for well over 40 years, I can relate to the feather-chewing bird. Like nail biting in humans, feather chewing is an enigmatic problem that may resolve itself seemingly spontaneously or never correct at all. Usually, however, behavioral feather chewing or self-mutilation can be at least partially or seasonally corrected with the help of a behavioral history, environmental manipulations, improved training, and distraction from the vice.

Begin with a trip to an avian veterinarian. The chewing of feathers may arise from disease processes or nutritional deficiency, and the possibility of a physical problem is ever present. While feather chewing that is related to the desire to breed is technically a hormonal problem, or rather related to stress generated by hormone activity, it can often be successfully treated with behavioral techniques. Even though feather chewing in many individual birds may be traced to a physical or disease origin, I believe that most feather chewing in healthy birds will respond once the physical problem is remedied if sound behavioral modifications are begun promptly at the onset of the problem.

While it is not unusual for a normal healthy parrot to pluck out a feather or two, particularly during molting, a self-mutilating bird might remove all breast, primary wing, or tail feathers in one sitting. The surprised owner sometimes returns to the room to find a bare-breasted bird and a pile of feathers on the floor or bottom of the cage. I once saw a Goffin's cockatoo chew off every breast feather in 20 minutes when a noisy Patagonian conure was introduced two rooms away in a very large house.

It is generally agreed that behavioral chewing of feathers probably arises from some form of stress. The stress may be caused by worn, injured, or damaged feathers; incomplete molt; improper cage, height, or location; diet; handling patterns; bathing patterns; inappropriate light periods; lack of physical or mental stimulation; isolation; or temporary or permanent loss of an owner (abandonment). If the source of the stress can be identified and removed quickly, the problem usually resolves itself spontaneously. For example, a parrot may chew its feathers every year when it is left behind for the family vacation and discontinue chewing when the family returns.

Once feather chewing appears, immediate steps must be taken to ensure that this stress reaction does not become habitual. Long-term feather chewing can damage feather follicles beyond their ability to regrow healthy feathers. The longer feather chewing continues, the more difficult it is to break. At this point the behavior is defined as a "vice," an ongoing fault. As a vice, it can easily be taught by one bird to another; indeed this is one of the hazards of boarding birds. I once saw a beautiful blue and gold macaw—who was, of course, also feeling abandoned—learn feather chewing from an African gray in the next cage while being boarded in a veterinary clinic.

Admittedly, it is *sometimes* helpful to provide a like-species companion bird in a separate cage. The presence of another bird alone is occasionally sufficient to stimulate the bird to discontinue feather chewing. The birds should not be housed together or be allowed together unsupervised, as a parrot that is chewing its own breast feathers will often chew the head feathers off a companion bird. I do not usually recommend this as therapy if the habit or vice is well established, although a companion bird can sometimes be successful in rehabilitating the new feather chewer acting from a

The Goddess Athena (left) had chewed off most of her feathers, yet she attracted her handsome mate Caesar (right), who preferred her to a younger hen in perfect feather.

sense of abandonment. Also, one must be ever watchful that the second bird is not learning the vice from the feather-chewing bird.

Begin the quest for a fully feathered parrot by taking a behavioral history. When was the onset of the chewing behavior? Was there some environmental change at that time? Was the bird appropriately caged? Was the bird trained to step up or socialized not to scream, bite, or chew? Was the bird provided with opportunities to make choices? Was the bird deprived of sleep? Deprived of interesting things to see, hear, and touch? Was the bird receiving a balanced diet? Was a child or another animal introduced to the home? Was the cage moved? Was the bird neglected or abandoned? Was the bird receiving too little or too much of some important nutrient such as protein?

Seasoned aviculturists have observed that the onset of feather chewing not infrequently accompanies a late or incomplete molt. Parrot behavior consultants such as Sally Blanchard, working as I do in the "laboratory" of the living room, have observed captive-raised babies begin feather chewing with damaged wing or tail feathers. These damaged feathers try to grow in but are repeatedly broken or chewed off. The source of these damaged feathers might be simple baby clumsiness; the chewing habit can be easily reinforced by lack of stimulation during the developmental period. A baby parrot with many broken wing and tail feathers, who is repeatedly breaking blood feathers, and "whining" and chewing the affected area should see an avian veterinarian immediately lest the practice become an established pattern.

Real or perceived abandonment frequently coincides with the onset of feather chewing. Self-mutilating behavior can often be traced directly to a family vacation, the return of an owner to work, change of ownership, or death of an owner. The very best way to prevent the onset of this behavior from these sources is proper socialization. The bird should not be encouraged to overbond to one person, but rather be provided with many opportunities for interactions and relationships with various humans. A conscious effort should be made to teach the bird to entertain itself.

Prepare a companion parrot for an owner's return to work by increasing quality time, perhaps sharing music, morning showers, grooming rituals, or exercise followed by short but gradually increased periods of isolation. A bathed and well-exercised bird will contentedly groom for a while, eat, and nap. If the bird is to be left alone all day, quality visual and sound stimulation can be provided with a television on a timer, set to come on a few hours before the owner returns from work. A television left on all day will interfere with the bird's nap time and desensitize the bird to the stimulation it provides. A few hours of game shows just before the owner returns home will also help to curb

screaming and attention-demanding behavior immediately after work. Of course the bird should have ample space. A bird that spends all day in a cage needs a larger cage than a bird who does nothing but sleep in its cage. A parrot housed only on an open perch without the security or climbing opportunities provided by a cage can easily develop feather chewing as well as several other problem behaviors.

An emotionally healthy parrot should have access to several toys, thereby providing opportunities for decision making. "Shall I go climbing now or play with my bell?" Having access to several behaviorally acceptable choices gives a companion parrot a greater sense of control and, therefore, security.

The vacation feather chewer may be corrected by taking the bird on vacation, improved technique by the in-home bird sitter, or by preconditioning for separation from owners with short visits to the location of the bird sitter. Not only should the bird sitter be experienced in the physical care of parrots; try to find a sitter that the bird likes.

Effective rebonding to a new owner is crucial in correcting the "abandoned" feather-chewing parrot. After at least two weeks of shared quality time spent feeding from the hand, bathing, eating, and sleeping in each other's presence, the bird should be taken on safe social outings where the new owner is the only familiar human. The new owner should take the bird to the groomer and the veterinarian, "rescuing" the bird from these frightening situations followed by rewards of cuddles (if the bird likes cuddles) or favorite foods. In extreme cases including anorexia in the abandoned or bereaved feather chewer, a professional behavior consultant can assist in rebonding with carefully executed psychodrama.

Purely behavioral feather chewing in young birds, particularly hand-fed birds, can easily appear during the developmental period. Stress caused by constant reprimands, lack of ac-

Birds that are chewed no more than this one often regrow feathers, sometimes even after several years of chewing.

cess to acceptable choices of behaviors, lack of understanding of what is expected, or understimulation during what should be an exciting, experimental time for the young parrot can easily lead to a life of chronic feather chewing. Feather chewing evolving during this important phase of a parrot's life is probably the most difficult type of chewing to correct, particularly if it has gone unchecked for many years. The remedy is to try to lead the bird through the period again. Encourage new emotional and intellectual development through increased training and stimulation while distracting the bird from the behavior. This must be done slowly and sensitively, particularly if the bird is over eight years old, as too much pressure to learn too quickly or too many environmental changes made too quickly can easily exacerbate the problem.

I am not an advocate of collars for the modification of behavioral feather chewing. If the bird is a new chewer, the stressing situation may not yet have been resolved and the additional stress added by the collar can increase the desire to chew or cause the bird to become ill. Collars are, I understand, helpful in treating self-

Packing the Cage

Presuming that the bird is in a cage it likes, in a location it likes; presuming that diet and exercise are adequate; presuming that there is no teasing by human or animal companions, the bird may often be distracted from habitual feather chewing by *"packing"* the cage.

Completely fill the cage with clean branches that have not been sprayed with either insecticides or herbicides. There should be so little space left in the cage that the poor bird can barely stand up completely straight or turn around without coming into contact with branches. The branches should be small enough so that the bird can easily chew them out of the way to make a space for its own body. They should have bark that can be removed as a form of entertainment by the bird. We are trying to distract the bird from the habit of feather chewing long enough to learn the more natural parrot behavior of "making toothpicks."

If the bird seems extremely stressed by even the slightest change in the environment, pack the cage gradually—a branch or two every day for a period of a week or two. If the bird continues chewing on feathers, add more branches. If the bird discontinues chewing on feathers, let the "bird-carved" space remain. Continue to provide lots of fresh new twigs in an easily accessible place.

mutilation caused by injury or a disease process.

Some birds enjoy "shredding" cotton or jute fibers. If a love for the disintegration of fabric is observed, provide a hankie or piece of fabric or two. It is always more effective if the bird is able to choose this object from a number of options that the bird itself discovers. For example, you might notice that Cecilia is crazy about that lavender bandana or poor old frayed antimacassar, so why not just donate it to the Cecilia cause. Monitor the bird initially to try to determine whether it is ingesting fibers, and be ever alert for really stringy fabric shedding threads that might entrap little toes and toenails.

I like Booda Bones and, of course, the perennial parrot favorite, shoelaces. There is no more enticing object to a parrot than the tip end of a shoelace. I believe that many feather-chewing birds could be quickly and completely rehabilitated if we could just afford to pack their cages daily with new shoelaces.

If the bird has not been previously traumatized by spraying as a punishment or some other negative association with water or spraying, bathing is excellent therapy for feather chewers. A *Bird Talk* article several years ago recommended adding a little Listerine Antiseptic Mouthwash to the water to anesthetize irritated skin. I believe this is beneficial for Pacific species —cockatoos, lories, and eclectus— probably because of the aromatic nature of the spray.

I have seen success regrowing feathers on chewing New World birds such as Amazons, conures, macaws, and pionus with the occasional addition to the spray bath of sea salt (the kind used for saltwater aquariums). Parrot expert Tony Silva reports that South American parrots go to clay banks and eat mineral-rich clay on a daily basis, and that natives believe the birds are easier to catch if deprived of this mineral source for a few days. Although the bird can absorb only a small amount of minerals through its very small area of exposed skin, I believe that the bird also receives some mineral enrichment from breathing the fine spray mist of salt water. However, Dr. Jerry LaBonde, an avian veterinarian practicing in Colorado, reports that benefits from additives to water are undocumented. He believes that improved feather growth probably comes from increased owner attention that accompanies more frequent bathing.

Timing, too, can work for or against the recovering feather chewer. I believe the very best time to begin to rehabilitate the behavioral chewer is springtime. Summer, the molting season, is the time of most rapid feather growth, and the owner's ability to see progress will serve to motivate continued efforts. A regrowing program begun in April will often yield a feathered bird by September. A recovering feather chewer may relapse occasionally, but time between incidents will become longer as the behavior is discontinued.

On the Shoulder

The practice of allowing a medium or large hookbill access to the shoulder upon demand is vehemently and adamantly discouraged by many long-time aviculturists and parrot behavior professionals. This is not because the parrot allowed regularly on the shoulder is "usually" dangerous or even "frequently" dangerous, but because of the very severe nature of potential injuries. It's fun to snuggle with Paco on my shoulder, but is it worth losing an eye? There remains the very real threat of permanent damage to the face and to personal effectiveness and self-esteem.

With the smaller domesticated parrots—budgies, cockatiels, and lovebirds—danger is minimal. Owners of Amazons are at great risk of severe

Some cockatiels, though, are so aggressive that they cannot be allowed on the shoulder. Pearl, our office bird, with Assistant Editor, Dionne Coakley.

injury, as are owners of macaws, African grays, and cockatoos, and to a lesser extent caiques, conures, and lories. I believe a noisy, nippy "shoulder bird" conure is a creature very often relegated to a back room for the rest of its life—a life which may be prematurely short as a result of neglect abuse.

Additionally, a responsible counselor in the handling of companion parrots must discourage the practice of allowing the parrot on the shoulder because the activity itself encourages the development of aggression (particularly in a poorly trained bird).

Like puppies, human-bonded, hand-fed baby parrots are awesomely sweet. Their "sweet, sweet baby" period may last much longer than a dog's; but just as with dogs, without prevention training, aggression is just down the road. A "shoulder bird" will begin expressing overt aggression against people and animals approaching its "shoulder human." This behavior is usually easy to correct during the developmental period when the jealousy is expressed to defend territory and define status. If this behavior is allowed to persist, the "shoulder bird" will eventually express displaced aggression against the "shoulder human" because it is so enraged by jealousy, which includes issues of status, protection, and sexuality.

Both overt aggression and displaced aggression escalate with maturity. If aggression by the bird against everyone but you is tolerated, there is a real possibility that someday that bird will express displaced aggression against you. Displaced aggression toward the primary person is often more violent than any previous incident of overt aggression toward others.

The injury in an initial incident of displaced aggression against the primary person is not always so severe but may be worse and may be permanently disfiguring. Injuries include but are not limited to damaged ear, eye, ripped-open lips that do not recover full movement, or broken nose, finger, or arm. I live in a sparsely populated region, but as a behavior consultant for companion parrots, I carry a pager and receive referrals from hospital emergency room personnel. I receive up to a half dozen calls a year from people who have just been stitched up following bad parrot bites and who may or may not admit they need help. Women more frequently report or acknowledge serious facial injuries inflicted by a companion bird. Whether this is a matter of culture, interpreta-

Displaced Aggression

The scenario in which an initial incident of displaced aggression against a primary human occurs typically goes something like this:

Although Mary Lou had lived with budgies and cockatiels for years, Paco was her first large hookbill. At the age of ten, this formerly hand-fed Bluefronted Amazon had been accompanying Mary Lou on outings to public schools, malls, and other educational events for eight years. While they had some behavior counseling through the developmental period, Mary Lou did not think it necessary to banish the baby from the shoulder, require him to respond dependably to the "Step-up" command, or house him below eye level.

Mary Lou lived alone but dated Terry, who took a hands-off approach with Paco because of past incidents of aggression. Mary Lou always found it rather amusing to see her 350-gram bird abuse her 180-pound boyfriend, who occasionally teased the bird.

Mary Lou took Paco, with wing feathers always meticulously trimmed, to and from the car on her shoulder. Carrying a portable perch and a bag of food treats and toys, she was walking out the door one morning when Terry leaned over to plant a good-bye kiss on her left cheek. Paco—on the right shoulder—screamed, fanned his tail, pinpointed his eyes, and in a blink ripped Mary Lou's right cheek open. The wound tore straight down from the outside corner of her eye, requiring 16 stitches. Miraculously, the eye was unscathed.

tion, or frequency of occurrence is unknown.

In my opinion, there is no such thing as a "safe" shoulder. There are, however, ways to minimize the danger. For example, there is a recognizable phenomenon that many parrots who are absolute bullies in their own territory are nice as pie in public. This accounts for the many beautiful macaws that provide photo opportunities for tourists in markets and beaches around the world. (These birds are usually perched at chest level or below, which inhibits the development of height-related aggression.)

A "safer" shoulder, therefore, is in a location about which the well-trained parrot is not territorial and is not in the presence of another bird, person, or object of whom the bird is jealous.

This away-from-home/good behavior phenomenon is sometimes used to defend the reputation of a parrot who is charged with being "vicious" in its own territory. A friend of a friend of mine who had an absolutely charming blue and gold macaw lived in a small apartment building. In that building on the same floor level lived a man with a cat. There were no screens on the windows, and if the man with the cat left his window open and the man with the macaw left his window open, the cat would go in and harass the macaw. Of course, there was much animosity, because neither man could close his windows without the apartment's becoming uncomfortably hot. One day, the macaw owner returned to his almost all-white apart-ment to find it reduced to a bloody mess. Examination of the macaw cage revealed part of a cat's foot in the bottom of the cage.

I do not believe the cat survived, and the macaw owner was charged with keeping a vicious animal in the city. The macaw owner sued the cat owner for property damage, and everybody went to court. Now the blue and gold macaw can be very intimidating to the uninitiated, and although it has the most dependable disposition of the common companion macaws, a blue and gold in a cage can defend its territory quite aggressively.

This bird was a perfect angel in court. He went readily and sweetly to anyone and was exonerated of his "self-defense" crime. He might not have fared so well if an Animal Control Officer in a uniform who knew little about parrot behavior had evaluated his disposition in his own territory, especially in the presence of a person, bird, animal, or object of which the bird was jealous.

Of course, a parrot with a poorly reinforced step-up response should *never* be allowed on the shoulder. A parrot that will refuse to step up and that runs around to the other shoulder or to the middle of the back is demonstrating a controlling behavior usually consistent with a bird that will bite.

A "shoulder human" is frequently the object of displaced aggression against the telephone. How dare Mom/Dad spend so much time with that thing on the shoulder? A safer "shoulder human" will put the bird down before picking up the phone.

As the parrot reaches sexual maturity, we will see an increase in hormonally induced hostility. Because these periods of hormone activity are probably stimulated by photo periods (the length of daylight hours), they will often occur on approximately the same date every year. If you are the victim of a nasty hormonal rage, mark the date on your calendar and transfer it to your new calendar next year. Discontinue any shoulder time and be especially watchful for aggressive behavior beginning a week or two before the documented date of last year's aggressive behavior.

It is a good practice to wear eyeglasses when allowing the bird on the shoulder, particularly during the time of anticipated increased aggression. If the bird is stimulated to express overt or displaced aggression toward the face, it may bite the glasses instead of flesh.

Effective long-term behavioral groundwork, including well-established dominant status over the bird, will allow you some "safer shoulder" time through the bird's first ten years. Many—probably most—macaws,

Amazons, and African Grays over the age of ten years should not be allowed *any* shoulder time. I Repeat: real danger may be infrequent, but the risks are *very great!*

Chapter 6

Aggression

Teaching a Parrot to Bite—

Reinforcing Instinctive Behaviors Can Produce a Dangerous and Unlikable Bird

Nature produces the parrot's tendency to use its hard, sharp beak to bite. It is a tendency that possibly blossoms to fruition frequently in captivity. Humans and a poorly planned captive environment can easily reinforce the tendency to bite. An understanding of the parrot's instinctive behaviors combined with aggression-prevention handling mannerisms, a well-designed environment, and planned responses to the bird can reduce a parrot's natural tendency to bite.

I see several instinctive behaviors that probably generate the initial bite: crankiness, the flocking instinct, territorialism (see pages 105–108), and sexual-related aggression (see pages 108–113). Combine these with provocative behaviors by humans, unintentional reinforcement, and misunderstanding of how the bird uses the beak and you have a biting parrot.

The flocking instinct often contributes to the development of biting in a young parrot that interacts regularly with more than one person. Because sick or injured group members might attract predators, a "good citizen" of the flock might naturally try to drive the weaklings away. In family settings this perceived "weakling" might be the nicest person in the family, the smallest person, the quietest person, the oldest person, or another pet.

Of course, in human society, attacking "weaklings" is an extremely inappropriate behavior. In birds it must be socialized out by denying reinforcement, by providing responses that the biting bird does not want, and by teaching acceptable alternative behaviors to replace the undesirable behavior. One must be careful not to unintentionally reinforce any form of hard biting on humans or other animals.

Many varied responses will be interpreted by the bird as **reinforcement of the bite.** I usually presume that reinforcement of a negative behavior is unintentional; although I have seen resentful or hostile humans openly reward companion parrots with kisses, praise, or food rewards following a bite or attempt to bite a spouse, parent, sibling, or other pet. This can lead to dangerous tendencies in the bird that will not always be expressed against the person one might wish . It is a form of "behavioral bird abuse." A domestic hand-fed parrot that has been reinforced to bite matures into a vicious, dangerous creature with an uncertain, probably unhappy future.

An attacking parrot can easily be reinforced with **laughter** on the part of the favorite person. Although the behavior is self-rewarding (done for the pleasure of doing it), laughter from the favorite person could well be the next most sought-after response by the bird. And not laughing is very difficult! Here is a clumsy creature, who can't hold its bell and look at the food dish at the same time without falling off the perch, trying to kill someone 100 times its size! Laughing the first time the baby bird attacks your significant other is setting a dangerous precedent of reinforcing violence. We know it's not funny if our 14-month-old child tries to kick the dog; and we wouldn't permit, much less reinforce that behavior. A companion parrot has many of the same aggressive reactions as a human toddler; it is just as inappropriate to reinforce them in a parrot as it is in a human.

A more appropriate response to the stimulus is a stern look; a loud "Stop it!"; a wobble correction (see page 24), even if you have to pick the bird up to accomplish the correction; a loud clap of the hands, step-ups,

aerobics, or "time out" (wherever the bird *doesn't want to be* — for a hand-fed bird that might be the cage or the bathtub).

If abusive behavior against "weaklings" is tolerated or reinforced, a competitive parrot may later begin challenging perceived "strong rivals." If human attacking behavior is reinforced or tolerated, the sexually maturing parrot will later seek to dominate prospective mates and repel rivals.

In many parrot types, courtship begins with a "testing" or "battle of the wills" in which the individual parrots evaluate each other's strength and establish roles. It is not unusual for growing sexual urges to stimulate this behavior against even the primary person, but this behavior is still not nearly so dangerous and dramatic as displaced aggression generated by jealousy.

Simple **crankiness** on the part of a baby parrot can start a cycle of biting that is easily unintentionally reinforced. Following is one way this might begin:

TzaTza is going through his first molt. It must be an emotionally intense time for a six-month-old quaker. Last month he looked like a

It is very easy to reinforce biting behavior in most conures.

little round green satin apple. This month he looks like a lawn that was "mowed" with scissors.

He is moody, confused. He wants to be petted, but his neck is so full of stiff, new pinfeathers that he bites when I touch it. I have given up trying to accommodate the pets he still begs for, but I spend a lot of time kissing his little beak and blowing into his neck. He seems to enjoy both, closing his eyes like a cat squinting in the sunlight.

Sometimes he is quieter than usual. He is defensive of his cage. Yesterday, he bit my nose when I had a white cosmetic mask on my face and approached him too quickly.

Both of these bites were responses to stimuli from the human. These bites are best avoided by altering the behavior that stimulated them. A cranky baby parrot with a head and neck covered with stiff pinfeathers may seek comfort, but petting those pointy little pinfeathers will bring only a response to pain. Better to give the bird a bath to soften the feather sheaths. A nip by a cranky baby who got poked in the neck with a pinfeather, I believe, is best ignored, or perhaps petting should be discontinued until the feather condition clears up. As a matter of fact, most early bites from hand-fed baby birds are probably accidents. Consequently, most nibbles and accidental bites are best completely ignored.

The nip on the nose by the baby sitting on its cage can be treated with a stern look, a loud, "Cut it out," and a swift lockup inside the cage below. Prevent the nip on the nose by

- avoiding the cranky bird if your appearance is not usual (cosmetic mask, new glasses, sunglasses, hat, etc.);
- "prompting" the bird's good mood by saying "good bird," before you prompt for physical contact;
- approaching more slowly. Quick movements are, more often than not, the culprit here. Fast movements are for the one under authority, not for the one in charge.

Accidental reinforcement also includes pulling back every time the bird puts its beak on the hand. This will cause the bird to believe that the perch is unsafe. It will respond by more aggressively "testing" the potential perch before stepping up. The behavior of putting the beak on the hand before stepping up must be ignored if the bird is to trust the perch (hand) and respond dependably to the prompt to step up.

Poking and pointing at a bird with quick movements are extremely provocative. This is a problem for people who are animated talkers. Waving or wagging fingers swiftly in the bird's face is interpreted by the bird as an invitation to fight, particularly if those fingers are enhanced with brightly colored fingernails. While many birds really enjoy being petted with long fingernails (they feel like a beak!) and can tolerate brightly colored fingernails, if biting persists, one really must examine the way those fingers are being presented to the bird. A pointed appendage —finger, toe, or nose—approaching quickly into the bird's face is an almost irresistible stimulus to bite.

Don't "thump" the bird on the beak: This is ultimately a counterproductive act. I believe it is a little too enraging not to inspire grudges that will be avenged when the opportunity presents itself.

Many bites are either accidental or a matter of interpretation. Don't overreact. An accidental bite unintentionally reinforced or responded to with much drama can easily become a permanent habit.

Territorialism in Young Parrots

No companion animal is more aggressive than a parrot who loves too much. Whether the bird is overbonded to a cage (location) or a person (perceived mate), intruders are chased rudely away. Even some of the smallest hookbills can scare an intruding human half to death.

A parrot may be "territorially overbonded" to a location, cage, or person; or may be "sexually overbonded" to a human who is a perceived mate. Both behavior patterns may be seasonal, but the former is present in both young and mature birds, while the latter is seen in mature birds. The ability to modify the behaviors depends upon the age and history of the bird and the sensitivity and cooperative skills of human companions.

Suppose your True Love purchased for you the ultimate gift: a beautiful, outrageously expensive parrot that bubbled with enthusiasm whenever you talked and apparently wished for nothing more than to live and be loved by you. But within a few months, the bird was lunging angrily when you walked by and was infatuated with your significant other. Within another few months, it seemed that the bird wanted to either kill you or drive you out of your own home. This kind of "love triangle" can be emotionally devastating to even the strongest individual.

To overcome bonding-related aggression, one must first determine whether the bird is acting out of territorialism or sexuality. Many territorially motivated behaviors are similar to sexually motivated behaviors, although the former are substantially easier to modify.

If the behaviors are territorial, even though the bird will obviously cling to and protect *one* chosen person, there will be no history of regurgitation for only the chosen human (many baby parrots try to feed each other), no *excessive* wood chewing, and (in the case of Amazons and macaws, in particular) no strong "parrot musk" smell associated with a mature parrot in sexual overload. There will usually be tail displays and pinpointing of eyes. There may be attacks upon everyone except the favored human, with particular ferocity toward the human mate of the bird's perceived human "territory."

While it is difficult not to "flirt" with a talking, eye-flashing, and tail-displaying parrot, these behaviors should not be reinforced. In particular, no matter how funny it is to see a little bird terrorize a grown human, we must never laugh when Paco tries to kill our better half. This is surely a form of "spouse abuse" that reinforces the bird to attack.

We know that the smaller the territory over which the bird has control, the more intense the efforts to control that territory. This concept also applies to people. Generally speaking, the fewer people with whom the parrot interacts, the more passionately the bird will try to control this "human territory" by fending off intruders. In a family of five, the parrot might not let the spouse into the kitchen. In a family of two, the parrot might try to kill the spouse whenever it has the chance.

Treating territorial overbonding involves establishing a "commuter" life-

African Senegals often develop territorial behavior.

style for the bird by removing the cage to an unfamiliar area in the home (making that area into a "roosting area") and providing a portable play area or basket with an appropriately perch-sized handle, so that the bird may have a moving "foraging area." Several play areas in various parts of the house can be provided with the use of unpainted baskets with handles (wrap the basket handle with jute or heavy twine for durability). If there are other pets in the house, it might be a good idea to hang the baskets from the ceiling. Of course, each "foraging area" should be outfitted with toys, food, and water dishes.

The companion parrot's behavior is improved by outings into unfamiliar territory: visits to the vet, a friend's house, a friendly pet store, or public event. Dominance-prevention techniques such as retaining the bird on the hand—the Egyptian grip (see page 22)—should be used at home. Although a typical parrot *will* develop aggressive behavior solely as a result of being allowed to "hang out" on the favorite human shoulder, most parrots will not display aggressive behavior only as a result of being on the shoulder in *unfamiliar territory*. Visits to strange places improve the bond between the bird and *any* familiar human—particularly the perceived rival.

If aggressive parrot behavior is truly the result of sexual overload, treatment is more complicated, as we will discuss later. Early prevention training is necessary for good social adjustment in mature birds. I believe the chances of favorably modifying aggressive behavior resulting from territorialism in a young parrot are very good, probably better than 95 percent. Modifying true sexually motivated aggression in most hookbills between 8 and 30 years old is more difficult, but may be accomplished much of the time if adequate early training has been provided. The bird may not be handleable during its breeding season, but will be fine the rest of the year.

Aggression in the Mature Parrot

Sexuality is probably the single greatest cause of aggression in mature companion parrots. During the 1980s, about a third of the parrot behavior problems I saw were related to strong, sexually-motivated bonding—often referred to as "overbonding"—to a person, another bird, or a reflection.

Territory, height, and strong attraction have an intoxicating effect on a companion parrot's behavior. They are exhilarating, provocative. Being overly attracted to any of these elements is similar to becoming addicted to a drug. The overwhelming desire to control these treasured elements often brings some very uncomfortable side effects, particularly on the disposition of a parrot. An overbonded parrot will use intimidation and violence to retain control of every element of its physical and emotional territory.

A mature hormonal parrot allowed to become very territorial is a pugnacious martinet, prone to fits of anger, jealousy, spitefulness, venge-fulness, and overt, passive, and displaced aggression. But there is more here than simple anger; there is cunning. A parrot can hold a grudge for a *very* long time.

Overbonding takes on a violent tone when sexual hormones come into play. Some parrots exude a strong musklike odor, regurgitate for or on the object of their affection, display feathers, pinpoint eyes, reduce everything they can reach to confetti, and demonstrate dangerous aggression. An incident of violent aggression by a usually sweet bird exhibiting the above behaviors should be "charted" on a calendar. The aggressive behavior may recur on exactly the same date every year. I suggest special handling a week or two before the previously documented incident and a week or two after it during the reproductive years. During periods of peak hormonal activity in a large hookbill's teens and twenties, it is safest to handle the bird when you are wearing eyeglasses and using a hand-held perch.

Overt Aggression: Given the opportunity, a parrot will often attack the "other mate" of their very favorite person, that person's friends, children, or other pets.

Displaced Aggression: Sometimes, however, a parrot bites not because it dislikes the object of the bite, but because it likes that person too much. The best-loved person is very often the victim of displaced aggression. Parrots seem to subscribe to the concept: "When you're not near the one you want to bite, bite the one you're near." I have seen many severe human facial injuries that were the result of having a beloved companion parrot on the shoulder when a spouse walked into the room or when attention was paid to another parrot. Be ever watchful. This behavior may emerge spontaneously in a bird that has never before demonstrated aggression against the primary person.

Displaced aggression escalates with sexual maturity. If the bird attacks everyone but the primary person, someday it will attack the primary person. Displaced aggression toward the primary person is often more violent than any previous incident of overt aggression toward others.

"Passive" Aggression: Many mature parrots will sweetly entice a human with song, words, and gestures, and then bite when approached. If you see a strange parrot begging for your attention, but are told "Don't you believe it," trust the people who are warning you.

Controlling Overbonding: I believe many people obtain a parrot because they have a need to fill in their own emotional lives. I see women obtain a precious parrot when they lose a lover; I see men with new baby hookbills when their wives are nursing and bonding with human infants. But allowing a bird to become overbonded to only one person in a multiple-person household can be dangerous. Family members must coordinate their efforts to have a well-socialized bird that does not "pick on"

anyone in the family. Use of the "Egyptian" handling mannerisms (see page 22), consistent reinforcement of the step-up command, and fair attention to establishing human dominance (the effective authority-based relationship) will provide firm behavioral groundwork for a lifetime of successful social interaction with a parrot.

Height Factors: A parrot that is housed too high will often develop aggressive tendencies toward perceived "underlings." I have seen vicious Amazons turned into baby dolls by cutting only 5 or 6 inches (12–15 cm) off their cage stand. Height factors are particularly problematic in macaws. I receive many calls from people with toddlers and maturing juvenile macaws. I often go to the home to find a bird on top of a cage at a height that causes it to look up at the male companion and down at the woman and children. With a young macaw, if we can either lower the bird or raise the height of the wife and children, the behavior is often *instantly* corrected and can be permanently reinforced by use of the other techniques discussed in this chapter.

Commuting: A parrot's indulgence in territorialism may be modified by providing the bird with a commuter life-style. Parrots who stay in exactly the same place all the time often become temperamental and "bity" (that's about a half-a-mile past "nippy" and means that the bird is doing actual physical damage to human flesh). African grays and cockatoos have very strong tendencies to become overbonded to the cage, expressing either aggression or fear when anyone approaches the cage.

In the wild, except when nesting, most parrots probably sleep in *approximately* the same place every night then go away every day to forage in many places. Strong aggressive tendencies probably do not develop to as great an extent in the foraging territories as in the roosting territory.

I believe a pet bird is best allowed to roost in a cage in a fairly isolated part of the home at night, then be included in family activities at many communal "foraging" (play) areas during the day. The bird becomes dependent upon a person who physically takes it from the roost to the foraging areas. It is the task of the "less-liked" person to take the bird to "forage" every day. If the bird does not tolerate handling by this less-liked person, it is deprived of social interaction with the flock. The intelligent, manipulative parrot soon learns that social interaction with the less-liked person is necessary to get to the ones with whom it wants to be. The bird learns to enjoy social interaction with more humans.

I suspect that this transportation dependence is what parrot behaviorist Sally Blanchard is accomplishing with her training principle of never allowing the bird to climb out of the cage on its own. Although I have not heard that she advocates "roosting and foraging" in the manner recommended here, she develops the same dependency relationship by allowing the bird to leave the cage only on the human hand.

Outings: Outings into unfamiliar territory with less-than-favorite humans are particularly effective in the modification of aggression. A bird in a strange place in the company of strangers will most likely be very nice to any familiar person—even its most-hated rival. Social outings for parrots teach the bird that even when it is not in total control of the environment, life is safe and stimulating and the less-than-favored person becomes a soul mate. A parrot who goes on lots of outings will be sweeter and better adjusted at home as well as in public. Watch for signs of stress, and avoid allowing the bird on the shoulder in the car, as unexpected behaviors can cause accidents. Some people allow the bird to sit on a small cage, perch, or basket and look out the window. The safest transportation is in a rigid carrier secured with a seat belt.

Exercise: A healthy bird is an active bird. A parrot must be provided with sufficient exercise (see pages 76–79). I believe many incidents of aggression can be averted if the bird has adequate physical exercise.

Preferred Handling: The less-than-favorite person should have the opportunity to handle the bird in desirable situations. Going to the play area, to the shower (if the bird likes to bathe), to the TV room, and to the dinner table are excellent opportunities for the bird to be reinforced for good behavior toward a perceived enemy who is providing transportation. Many birds that are usually absolute "vampires" are sweet as can be when they are wet. It's a perfect opportunity to work on handling skills.

Abhorred Handling: The very favorite person has the responsibility of performing less desirable tasks with the bird—bathing the bird that hates bathing, reprimanding misbehavior, perhaps even grooming. Although a shy bird is best groomed professionally, I believe some Amazon and macaw owners establish dominance very well by grooming the bird at an appropriate moment. A nippy bird with a sharp upper mandible can often be taught not to bite by keeping an emery board handy enough to file a bit off the beak tip *immediately* after a bite.

Hormone Therapy: In addition to training and aggression-prevention adjustments in the environment, hormone therapy is available from an avian veterinarian. As with any drug therapy for behavioral reasons in humans, this is probably a treatment of last resort and should be undertaken only with great care.

I have many times seen parrots switch from persecuting a person to loving that person as a result of a rescue. If a bird is picking on a particular person, that is the person who should "rescue" Paco from perceived danger. Watch for naturally occurring opportunities, such as the groomer or veterinarian. It may not work the first time or two, but if you take advantage of every opportunity, this technique can really turn a relationship around. A practicing bird behavior consultant may be able to assist you in setting up an artificial rescue scenario. This is best done only with expert supervision.

Changing Loyalties: If you are handling a parrot to compensate for overbonding, watch for signs of changing loyalties and adjust the behaviorism program accordingly. A parrot may switch favorites from time to time.

It happens with people, too. For 13 years growing up in a small town, I watched my mother interact socially with a group of about 20 very parrotlike women. I got to watch their relationships evolve. One year Mom would be close with Mrs. A—best buddies, bridge partners, and confidants. The next year they were worst enemies, wouldn't play bridge at the same table, and acted like strangers when forced to come face to face in our small community.

Meanwhile Mom would be really close with Mrs. B—shopping and telephone buddies and, of course, bridge partners, until the inevitable falling out. Then Mom would have a close relationship with Mrs. C, until one day she would wake up and realize that her *real true friend* was none other than Mrs. A! Then she would cycle through the whole community again.

A parrot in the house for many years is also likely to change alliances for almost any perceived "mistreatment" by a beloved human. Sometimes a change in alliance can be traced to a single incident—an accident during social interaction in which the bird is frightened or injured. A period of "abandonment"—a vacation or return to work—can trigger a change in loyalties by the parrot. The

Rescue Scenario

The animal rescue scenario, which occurs in fables from many lands, may be the oldest known animal behaviorism technique. It was taught to me by a Congo African gray, the first one I ever handled. The bird, with a reputation for pugnacity, was sitting in a cage on the floor of a pet shop for over a year. Two other tamers had tried unsuccessfully to socialize the bird. It was a Saturday afternoon, and there were many people in the store. Because the bird wouldn't come out, I removed the trays and dishes and turned the cage upside down, then watched as the bird went scooting down the aisle to a ferret cage. The ferret took one look and said, "Wow, dinner!," grabbed a toe, and started chewing. The bird was screaming, blood splattering, and people came running. I pried the ferret's teeth off the bird's toe and went to the corner. The bird was immediately my best buddy, submitting to petting and learning to step up in a matter of minutes, even though he had repeatedly resisted such training from others.

changing of alliances by a parrot isn't as sophisticated as the same process in my mother's group of bridge players. While Mom's friends merely ignored and snubbed one another, a sexually mature, overbonded parrot may *actually attack almost anyone, including the one it loves.*

A bird may change loyalties for no apparent reason, but may be responding to some mysterious life cycle. I believe I have observed emotional cycles of four years in large cockatoos. I know one umbrella cockatoo who loved his Mom and tried to kill his Dad for the first four years of his life, then loved his Dad and tried to kill his Mom until he was eight. Then at the age of eleven and a half he was showing signs of switching again, when the owners decided they couldn't handle him any more and set him up to breed.

Because of the configuration of the beak—with two points on the lower mandible and one point on the upper mandible—the cocaktoo can administer an extremely damaging and painful bite. This particular bird was quite intimidating and actually dangerous. It had been hand-fed, but its "natural" personality was allowed full latitude, and no aggression-prevention techniques were in place. At the age of 11 this enormous, beautiful, male umbrella cockatoo did not successfully respond to the initiation of behavioral training.

Just because a young baby bird is the "sweetest little thing you ever saw," doesn't mean it won't be dangerous when it reaches sexual maturity. This umbrella cockatoo might still be a pet today if "step-ups" had been sternly reinforced and aggression-prevention techniques had been begun sooner. As it is, he is proudly making very sweet babies, and I (almost) don't miss his affection. It is possible that his gentle disposition will return when his "breeding lifetime" is passed, and we will retrain him to be the sweet pet he was in his youth.

Occasionally we see grays and Amazons, particularly, double yellow heads and yellow napes, that cannot be handled at all for many years. However, some of those very ornery parrots that have terrorized humans for a generation or more might suddenly demonstrate a desire for human handling. I have recently seen several older birds do an about-face and become handleable after years of fierceness. I have, on several occasions, introduced companion birds, believed to be mean for many years, to happy relationships with new families or new generations of their longtime family. Although it lasts much longer than the terrible twos, I believe that the aggressive sexual hormone phase eventually passes.

If your winged terror has been a monster for years, but suddenly demonstrates different behaviors such as screaming for attention or begging, it may be ready to return to the "family affection fold." In time, even the worst vampire may respond to a little more training and a little more love.

Chapter 7

The Companion Parrot in the Human World

Reading Parrot Body Language

Because it is difficult to read a bird's facial expressions, observers of parrot behavior look for body language to evaluate how a parrot feels. A lethargic bird with puffed-up feathers is probably not feeling well. Recognizing a sick bird has often been described in other books, but here we will discuss how parrots communicate normal, healthy emotions. Sensitive owners observing wagging or flaring tails, flipping wings, wiggling tongues, tapping feet, and pinpointing eyes are reading signals about what their bird is feeling.

Tail Wagging

A wagging tail might be saying, "I'm glad to see you!"; "That was interesting!"; or "My tail feathers are out of place!"

This behavior is usually performed with exuberance and frequently follows a "puff up and head shake"—the mannerisms that are used for greeting a beloved friend entering the area.

Wagging the tail rapidly back and forth is common in many types of birds, including parrot-type birds. Some of the most frequent and vigorous tail waggers in the avian family are ducks and geese—water fowl—suggesting that perhaps the source of this behavior is shaking water from the tail. In the case of parrots, it is also observed in wet birds shaking water off their tails, as well as dry birds "shaking off" the remnants of their most recent experience.

The wag is usually described as a "termination behavior," which often occurs at the perceived end of one activity or the beginning of another. In my observation, in order for a tail wag to occur in a parrot, the experience was at least tolerable and probably was perceived by the bird as pleasant.

A tail wag is also something like a giggle. Athough it might be occasionally absent in a happy creature, it is often absent in an unhappy one. Tail wagging is no guarantee of happiness and health, for even a sick, unhappy individual might occasionally express a nervous giggle. This behavior, like any other, must be evaluated within the context of all the bird's behavior.

When called for an evaluation, one of the things I look for is the presence or absence of tail wagging. In a previously unhandled bird (import or parent-raised domestic) the appearance of at least one or two tail wags during the first 20 minutes of observation by a stranger in their territory can evidence developing satisfactory adjustment to the home.

An avian behavior consultant might begin a house call with a 20 to 40 minute observation and evaluation of the animal's behavioral adjustment to the environment. A second similar time period involves handling the bird to observe responses to stimuli and "training" to unfamiliar techniques to demonstrate what the bird is capable of. Finally, humans must be taught to perform the techniques and to reinforce acceptable responses.

During phase two of this process, I periodically place the bird on a perch, then sit lower than the bird and outside its personal space, watching for those tail wags. If I see a tail wag immediately or within the first 60 seconds after the bird has been handled, I know I can push the bird at least as far as it has been pushed, perhaps further. If the tail wag occurs one to two minutes after the bird is placed on the perch, I know that I should push no further. If there is no tail wag or if the tail wag comes more than two minutes after placing the bird on the neutral perch, I presume I have push-

These citron and Eleanora cockatoos are quite happy to see each other.

ed too hard, and I must back off a little the next time I handle the bird or change my approach entirely.

Several behavior problems I see in companion birds may be related to malaise or depression. Increasing tail wags, puff outs, and pinpointing are indications of developing success when treating such conditions as anorexia, overweight, inactivity, and failure to talk.

If we start by manipulating only the environment until we are seeing more tail wags, particularly if they are accompanied by decreasing wing flips, we are probably progressing —however imperceptibly to the casual observer— toward a happier, better socialized hookbill. We're talking "baby steps" here, but every journey begins with the first step.

Stretching

Although I agree with some people who believe that kitties invented yoga, there is no question in my mind that birds invented tai chi, the Chinese system of calisthenics and meditation practiced to produce body flexibility and peace of mind.

Most healthy parrots practice a series of gracefully choreographed stretching motions frequently. The shoulders might be raised in unison, followed by the mirror image motion of extending the other wing and foot in unison. The message communicated by a bird's stretching like this is one of well-being. The stretch is an "initiation behavior" that usually comes at the beginning of the day or the beginning of the time of day that a bird interacts with human comrades. It is most often observed when people first enter the room.

The stretch says, "See how glad I am to see you?" An appropriate response is to mimic the bird (if the bird doesn't understand your words yet) or to reply with "Yes, you are very, very pretty, and I am very glad to see you, too."

Preening

The tiny little barbs on the feather filaments resemble the teeth of a zipper. A clean, healthy-looking feather is perfectly zipped. A physically and emotionally healthy bird spends a good deal of time keeping those feathers properly zipped. Preening, or grooming the feathers, expresses a sense of safety and well-being; but more, it expresses the feeling: "I want to look nice for you." A bird preening while sitting on a hand could be a prelude to greater expressions of bonded interest from the bird.

Alopreening

When a bird feels compelled to preen human hair (head, facial, or otherwise) this is saying, "I like you; I want to help you look healthy and pretty for me." The appearance of alopreening from bird to human can signify a positive step toward an improved relationship.

A bird with a neck full of pin feathers with no avian companion to clean them off will depend on its human companion to remove the casing from pin feathers that it cannot reach itself. Instructions for this activity are found in "How to Pet a Parrot," page 27.

Bird Scratching Its Own Head, Chin, or Neck

A bird with a dazed, come-hither look who has head and neck feathers puffed up and is slowly scratching its own neck, chin, or head is saying "I'm so pitiful and lonely, I have to scratch my own self." This is clearly an invitation to pet: "Oh, Mom/Dad, won't you pleeeeease come scratch my head?"

Facial Feathers Fluffed Over Beak

In the presence of other aggressive signals, fluffed facial feathers might mean aggression; but within a peaceful context, face feathers fluffed over the beak is usually an extremely coy expression. This is particularly true when combined with self-scratching.

This behavior is frequently practiced by cockatoos who are saying, "I'm so sweet, I don't even have a beak."

I have seen a few cantankerous birds who will entice an unsuspecting stranger with this compelling look, and then bite them. Some of these creatures are little "con artists." If the human companion says "Don't believe the look, the bird's a vampire!," it is probably safest to believe the human companion. I have, however, occasionally encountered birds that hated the owner and bit the owner whenever possible, but loved everybody else. This situation is even more unhealthy than a bird that bites everyone but the owner.

Beak Grinding

This behavior says, "I'm going to sleep now." A normal, healthy hookbill rubs the lower mandible against the inside of the upper mandible, eyes closing, standing on one foot. I believe this is a grooming activity that keeps the birds lower beak sharp and ready to eat upon waking. A bird that has been very depressed for a long time might omit this behavior, with subsequent overgrowth of the lower mandible. This condition might also be accompanied by ill health. The sudden appearance of an overgrown beak is certainly a reason for a veterinary consultation, followed by a behavioral consultation if no health problems are found by the avian veterinarian.

Sleeping on One Foot

While this is a healthy behavior, suddenly noticing that the bird is spending a lot of time on one foot might mean that the bird is sleeping more than usual, which might indicate ill health.

Wing Flipping

I also look for flipping or slapping wings against the body when evaluating parrot behavioral adjustment. Wings might be flipping in anger, frustration, or because a feather is out of place. The bird might be in pain, or it might be settling down for sleep. A bird that is flipping its wings is not seeking interaction and may be threatening impending aggression.

A parrot that has flipped one wing once has said, "Watch it, I'm not sure I'm ready for this." A parrot that has flipped each wing once has said, "I'm really quite over this." A parrot that has flipped both wings more than twice is either in pain or very agitated: "If you mess with me, you'll be sorry!" If the bird is large and the behavior is accompanied with pinpointing eyes or a flaring tail it is absolutely unwise to handle the bird at this time.

If most conditions are adequate, I think a companion bird with a frequent hostile, wing-flipping attitude, particularly when accompanied with flashing eyes, fanning tail, and in some cases a strong "parrot musk" odor probably needs more baths. Call it a "cold shower" or call it "raining in the jungle"; frequent animosity even passively expressed against peaceful companions is often accompanied by aggression and is unnecessary and unacceptable. If the angry, hostile, wing-flipping bird's enviornment, diet, and social patterns seem adequate, the bird may need more outlets to express energy. That might mean exercise or baths. The energy required to recover from a drenching rain shower probably prevents much non-food related aggression both in the jungle and in the living room.

Just as I count increasing tail wags as an indication of approaching success when treating depression-related behaviors, I count decreasing wing flipping as an indication of developing success when treating established aggression in a companion hookbill.

Whether a parrot is sedentary or aggressive, the frequency of these two behaviors can be an indication of regression or progress toward behavioral goals. If we observe more wing flips than tail wags every day, we may be seeing a bird that is not happy in its enviornment, and the bird's human companions probably have justi- fiable reason to be less than thrilled with the bird's behavior.

Tongue Wiggling

This is most frequently and obviously observed in cockatoos and cockatiels, but is also seen in other types of parrots. Some people call this "beak chattering." It involves holding the upper and lower mandibles slightly apart and moving them up and down very quickly, combined with an apparent movement of the tongue in and out in a sort of "licking" or "tasting" motion. This behavior is probably translatable as "YumYum-YumYumYumYum."

In human terms this is an expression of affection: "I like it!" or "I like you!"

This behavior is frequently accompanied by a fluff out and tail wag.

Pinpointing

The narrowing of the pupil and enlargement of the iris—sometimes called "flashing"—is easily seen in a light-eyed parrot. This behavior, which is probably present but difficult to observe in dark-eyed birds, it is frequently observed in species known for facility in acquiring human speech —yellow napes, grays, yellow fronts, conures, and macaws. While it is not unusual to see a parrot that pinpoints but does not talk, with the exception of dark-eyed birds, I have never taken a history of a parrot-type bird that talks that does not also exhibit an observable iris movement.

If we are trying to teach new words, the appearance of flashing eyes is a

sign that this is an excellent time to model the words we want the bird to learn. But pinpointing is probably more an indication of motivation than an indication of talking ability.

Pinpointing is sometimes an indication of motivation to violence and frequently accompanies the flaring tail and stiffly extended shoulders of the courtship display. If we are unfamiliar with the bird or know or suspect that the bird has an uneven disposition, this is an excellent time to allow the bird some personal space.

Foot Tapping

This is another behavior that is common in cockatoos and occasional in other parrots. I believe foot tapping is usually a response to the perceived invasion of personal space and is usually a display of intended strength, dominance, or well-being. A rocking, foot-tapping cockatoo maintaining eye contact is saying, "You are standing too close to my perch, and this (tap, tap, tap) is *my* perch!"

Foot tapping is often a bluff. Just as the grouchiest gray is often not truly aggressive, the biggest-looking cockatoo with the grandest foot-tapping display might be the biggest baby. That is not to say, ignore the threat. If I don't know a bird, I treat this behavior and all other threats of aggression as the real thing.

Foot tapping in a tame umbrella or Moluccan cockatoo is really quite often a "drama game." Indeed, I suspect that they may have some type of code that facilitates communication by tapping back and forth. A tapping interaction can sometimes be initiated by a human tapping a pencil across the room, and is sometimes initiated by an interested cockatoo seeking some quiet attention. This tapping back and forth behavior might even be a quiet version of what Debbie Kesling calls a "contact call"—an unintrusive way for the codependent cockatoo to establish that its companion is safe and available. The playful form of this behavior was discussed previously in the chapter on games (see page 19). There is evidence to suggest that some cockatoos, such as the black palm, carry a stick around and tap on things with it as a part of their courtship rituals.

Flaring Tails

Unlike the pinpointing of eyes that may occur at moments of "normal" excitement, flaring tails demand ultimate respect. A flaring tail is a sign of exceptional excitement—such as sexual excitement—that is often ac-

This female eclectus is giving quite a decidely aggressive message. Compare her with the eclectus hen on the following page.

companied by aggression. While one might continue to handle a well-known bird with pinpointing eyes, even a familiar bird may be on the verge of expressing aggression when a flaring tail accompanies the pinpointing eyes.

Begging

A parrot that is staring intently (at someone or something) with its body flattened out, with quivering wings held out at the shoulders, is saying "Gimme!" This is the same behavior in parrots as the classic begging behavior in dogs: standing on hind legs, front paws folded to chest. It is similar to the invitation-to-breed/solicitation stance in female parrots; but begging is usually more animated and less strident.

A female eclectus begging.

Misinterpreted Messages

Most parrots cannot verbally communicate their feelings to humans. They must rely on body language to tell us how they feel. Parrot behaviors are frequently misunderstood by new owners who are unaccustomed to their ways. I have seen many otherwise caring humans try to stop their birds from vocalizing normal exuberant parrot song. I have seen humans punish their birds for trying to talk during periods in which they were also trying to teach talking. Parrots have no vocal cords; they must practice making different sounds. Some parrots practice new sounds softly; some birds really blurt them out. Parrots are vocal. If all the bird's needs are being met, the sounds we are hearing are probably expressions of delight and appreciation.

I have also seen quite a few new owners say that their bird "acted aggressive" when they tried to give it a spray bath. Often, when we reenacted the spray bath scenario, we saw a normal, happy bird exuberantly enjoying the water.

I believe miscommunication between humans and their avian companions directly contributes to many parrot "behavior problems." If there is behavioral maladjustment in a parrot, the solution is often found in enhancing human ability to understand the bird.

Parrots and Children

Many children have allergies or live in a setting where cats or dogs are unwelcome. If the rest of the family has a tolerance for noise (bird song), feathers, and a little mess, then birds can find a happy niche in their family "flock."

It is well documented that people talk more to their birds than to any other type of companion animal. While owners of companion birds don't always experience the physical closeness we feel with a dog or cat who might share our bed, I believe we are intellectually closer to our avian companions than we are to their less communicative mammalian cousins. Because of this close verbal and intellectual interaction, I believe parrots are excellent companion animals for children, particularly for an only child.

Depending upon the temperament and disposition of the child, one might choose to begin with the inexpensive and readily available American parakeet, or budgie. It is said that movie producer Steven Spielberg received the inspiration for his famous movie "ET, the Extraterrestrial" from free-flying budgies that inhabited his boyhood room. Although these colorful little creatures are every bit as smart as many other parrots, and more charming and beautiful, they are fragile and not particularly long-lived. I see many would-be juvenile aviculture careers cut short by the untimely, accidental death of one of these sweet, lovely creatures. It can be an emotionally devastating, guilt-inducing experience for a sensitive child, who might then avoid birds for life.

Lovebirds and cockatiels are great for careful children, but I prefer to see youngsters, particularly rambunctious ones, with a somewhat sturdier bird. My favorite bird for children is the

It may take a little practice to learn the "Egyptian" grip, but the improved responses from the bird are well worth the effort.

121

The Quaker, or monk parakeet, is an excellent bird for children. However, they may not be kept as pets in several states.

Quaker parakeet. These little companions are easily bred and relatively inexpensive in the areas where they are available. They are noisy but seldom aggressive. My second favorite is the brotogeris family—the gray cheeked parakeet or the canary-winged bee bee—followed by the pyurria family, then aritinga and other common conures.

For the bird's safety, a companion bird acquired for a child must be considered a family responsibility. It's a good idea to provide lots of behavior training and backup care for the first bird. It is also wise to have a standing appointment with a groomer so that the bird never has the opportunity to grow enough wing feather for flight. In addition to fly-aways, common and predictable dangers for children's birds are drowning in a glass or the toilet, being slammed in a door, being closed in drawers, being sat on, stepped on, or rolled on.

Sharing life with a bird provides children with opportunities to develop a sense of responsibility, decision-making abilities, and leadership potential. With a reasonably sturdy bird and a little planning, the benefits outweigh the risks. I have seen many youthful bird lovers grow into fine, responsible young adults.

Parrots and Other Pets

Because birds are social by nature, and because they relate to their group of companions—regardless of shape—it is not unusual for parrots to have lasting meaningful relationships with other pets. Although the predatory nature of some carnivorous pets can be hazardous to birds, sensitive introductions and pet "family planning" can ensure animal harmony in the home. Supervision of the new relationship as well as a carefully timed squirt or bop on the too-interested nose will guide an established, well-adjusted dog or cat to happy acceptance of a new bird in the home. Watch out for provocative behavior and establish limits the animals can understand.

People are often surprised to learn that I have both cats and birds. Indeed, one of the questions most frequently asked of a bird behavior consultant is, "Is it okay to have a cat with a bird?"

The answer depends upon the bird(s) and the cat(s). A macaw or other large parrot can easily handle almost any domestic feline, but a small finch or budgie may be lost to even a slightly predatory cat. Actually, bird-initiated aggression toward the other pets is at least as problematic as aggression from the other pets.

Aviculturists possessing large collections of birds frequently have stores of foodstuffs and grains that are attractive to rodents. A cat is a logical addition to such an environment and performs well as natural rodent control. A cat introduced to companion birds as a young kitten usually becomes completely trustworthy with *the kind of birds it was raised with*. Also, it is not necessary to starve a cat to induce it to catch mice. I suspect that kitties that don't go after birds may demonstrate increased enthusiasm for hunting mice.

As later discussed, a cat is a welcome diversion for alleviating boredom for a companion parrot that spends the day alone. Avian and feline pets form warm, playful, and sometimes romantic relationships. My cockatiel, Pearl, is often observed "soliciting" (with sexual postures) either her bell or her favorite kitty.

Adoring birds sometimes groom cat whiskers and fur, but I believe the most common bird-initiated cat play is "Come to me, come to me, go away." In this game the bird calls the cat (many birds literally use "here, kitty, kitty"), displays for the cat, hangs upside down to attract the cat, then bites, bops, or threatens kitty when it comes near.

My kitties like to steal toys dropped by Kaku, the cockatoo, whose favorite pastime is unhooking her numerous toys and dropping them to attract the kitties. Once the kitties are stationed under the cage investigating what toys have recently been dropped there, they are then "bombed" with other toys from above.

Cats are attracted to the smell and movements of birds. Smaller birds are more enticing because of their fluttering. When adding a bird to a home with cats, parrots—particularly larger ones—have the advantage. They are less attractive because they flap their wings with more decisive, less frenetic actions. Their hard beaks, intimidating size, domineering personalities, and naturally loud voices provide all the built-in socialization needed to protect from and usually dominate or befriend any domestic feline.

If it appears that a kitty is "stalking" the bird, a couple of squirts of water

A cat introduced to birds as a young kitten usually will remain trustworthy around the species with which it was raised.

directed at the kitty's face will terminate the kitty's interest immediately. A kitten squirted for inappropriate attention only a few times will usually discontinue "stalking" interest in a pet bird. With very little encouragement well-fed kitties usually forget their instincts to hunt birds. Although many cats can be trusted with even the smallest finches, canaries, budgies, lovebirds, and cockatiels, it is unwise to introduce smaller, soft-billed birds into homes with adult cats that have not been previously socialized to accept that kind of bird.

Keepers of small birds may acquire a very young kitten, training it to respect pet birds from that first awesome day in the new home. It is helpful for a large bird to "demonstrate" the need for respect with a supervised nip on kitten nose, ear, or tail; but usually a squirt or two of water carefully timed when feline attention is on the bird will convince the kitty that those feathers are off limits.

When adding a cat to an established "bird home," a trial visit by a "bird-socialized" kitty will demonstrate whether the bird likes cats. Although most pet birds are delighted and naturally curious, very rarely, a bird that has been previously traumatized by a cat may be emotionally unable to cope with one. Probably the smallest bird that can be successfully introduced into a home with a slightly predatory adult cat is a lovebird. These tiny pugnacious parrots can sometimes get the best of even a seasoned hunter. An acquaintance of mine says that in spite of great care on her part, the neighbor's Siamese cat gained access to her home and stalked her peachfaced lovebird playing in the kitchen sink. Hearing the sound of crashing pots, she found the poor cat streaking around the kitchen with an angry lovebird fiercely clenching his tail.

Probably the smallest bird that can be successfully introduced into a home with a predatory cat is the Quaker (about 5 ounces or 140–150 g). Noisy and somewhat nippy in multiples, these charming little clowns are excellent single birds who usually have no trouble dominating a mere domestic feline.

Years ago, I reluctantly recommended a Quaker to a friend with two very predatory cats. She was determined to rescue a plucked, stressed-out, bare-bellied Quaker. Imagine my surprise when I visited a few months later and found a fully-feathered parrot playing with the "hunters" and eating dry cat food out of their bowl on the floor!

Kitties who play with avian buddies should have their claws clipped regularly to prevent accidental (or on purpose) scratches. Even if the bird looks all right and acts all right, any bird whose skin has been scraped or punctured by a cat requires immediate antibiotic therapy (injectable ampicillin) from an avian veterinarian to prevent the development of pasteurella, a fatal bacterial infection.

While I find bird-socialized domestic felines to be excellent parrot companions, I do not believe a ferret can be trusted with *any* bird. They do not seem to be capable of changing their extremely predatory instincts against birds. I often hear of ferrets killing even large Psittaciformes such a cockatoos and macaws. Cockatiels, budgies, and lories haven't a chance.

Dogs and parrots also often form warm, devoted relationships; although an unfamiliar dog probably represents a greater danger to medium and larger hookbills than a cat. Because of the extreme differences between the many types and sizes of dogs, it is much harder to generalize about their behavior toward companion parrots. I have taken histories of dogs killing birds in instances of predatory aggression, overt aggression against the bird, and displaced aggression toward the bird in response to anger against some other person or situation.

Some of the "mouthier" types of parrots may be incompatible with barking or noisy dogs. Many parrots are at particular risk for developing abnormal screaming in response to barking dogs.

Introducing a dog into a bird home is thoughtfully preceded by a trial visit by a "bird-socialized" dog to determine whether the bird likes dogs. A bird that has been traumatized by a dog may be unable to tolerate one. I see many more parrots that fear dogs than parrots that fear cats. It is much easier to socialize young animals, although a well-adjusted older dog may accept a new bird immediately and without question. Because of the enormous variety of dog dispositions and temperaments, I believe the introduction of a dog into a home with a parrot should be made with the guidance of a dog behavior professional.

Reptiles usually represent minimal danger, although large snakes kept at liberty in the home can prey on pet birds. Pond and aquarium fish are not considered a threat to birds, although their aquatic environments are attractive and present a drowning hazard.

Although interspecies dangers exist and multiple-pet interactions should be well supervised, it is not unusual for companion pets to save each other's lives. Dogs have often alerted owners to dangers to pet birds just as birds often alert other pets and humans to dangers.

One of my clients, a student, shared a house near a university campus with several other students. The bird owner was well aware that Teflon fumes were poisonous to birds under certain circumstances, but had little control over the cookware used by his housemates. One night a roommate came home from an evening of beer drinking and decided to make spaghetti. After placing a pot of water on the stove, he fell asleep. Two hours later, the owner was awakened by the parrot calling out his name. Rushing downstairs, he found the Teflon coating on the pot in flames and was able to extinguish the fire. Although the bird saved the lives of humans and other pets, in this situation the bird did not survive.

The Bird Who Spends the Day Alone

One of the ironic elements of companion parrot ownership is that often when persons can finally *afford* that special large hookbill, they have to go to work all day in order to pay for it. Just as dogs left alone all day develop behavior problems, parrots left alone all day will, at the very least, be extremely demanding of attention in the evening. They may express anger through aggression, they may scream incessantly (or maybe just when you're on the telephone), they may begin chewing their feathers off, or destroying anything they can get their beaks on.

Just as children left alone all day can be expected to get into trouble, birds left alone all day can get into some surprising predicaments.

A bird that is left alone all day appreciates any companionship activities available. Breakfast is a traditionally shared meal. Morning grooming activities—bathing, showering or shaving, combing or blowing the hair dry—are excellent side-by-side activities to share with your parrot(s). If you have access to a telephone at work and a telephone machine at home, it's not a bad idea to call your bird to say "Hi!" or whatever other words you are hoping the bird will incorporate into its vocabulary. This serves the dual purpose of providing a little diversion during the

day and a little reinforcement for speech training.

A parrot is at particular risk for development of territorial aggression if it stays home all the time. It is highly desirable to take the bird on outings, perhaps to short work days, weekends in the country, or even simply to the shopping mall. Excursions, particularly with the less-than-favorite person, can help to ensure that the bird will not be phobic in new situations or with other people.

Just as it's a good idea to take your bird from window to window to show the bird the glass it might fly into, or from room to room while acclimating the bird to a new home, excursions to work will increase the bird's understanding of your behavior. An excursion to work will "demonstrate" to the bird that you have important "foraging" to do away from the "nest site."

If possible to accomplish safely, you may also choose to leave the bird alone in the work environment for a short time, maybe on a Saturday, so that it can see how boring that work environment really is. In a rare application of the "lesser of evils" training technique, the bird left briefly on a too-small-to-be-entertaining perch in a deserted office will see that there's something worse than being left alone in the stimulating, familiar home environment.

Another pet can also provide daytime diversions in the absence of human companionship. I think the easiest adjunct for this "ecological balancing" role is either a cat or an

Bird Versus Machine

One of my clients, an owner of two cockatoos, vacuumed her bird room every morning for several years with the same upright vacuum cleaner. Every day she left the vacuum cleaner in the same place in the sunroom where the birds lived at liberty. One day (maybe about the 700th day the vacuum cleaner had been sitting in that room) on her return from work she found that the birds had completely destroyed the vacuum cleaner. Apparently the vacuum cleaner parts were mostly plastic, and she affirmed that there was no piece left larger than 2 to 4 inches (5–10 cm) in diameter. The cockatoos had never touched the vacuum cleaner before.

aquarium within the bird's sight. An additional bird can easily cause jealousy, overt and displaced aggression, screaming, or several other negative behaviors as an expression of sibling rivalry by a bonded-to-a-human pet. Although dogs are excellent potential avian companions, they have many specialized environmental and training needs that make them more difficult to incorporate into the household.

A healthy parrot that has started the morning with bathing and grooming activity will spend a good amount of energy on that chore and will nap midday. Then, before Mom/Dad gets home, the bird can be awakened by a television on a timer.

Birds have excellent hearing and appreciate music, but eyesight is their most acutely-developed sense. Although the audio companionship of a radio is beneficial, I believe a bird given both sight and sound stimulation will be less demanding as a result of having more of its sensory needs met. Television is the easiest way to provide this stimulation in the owner's absence. Someday someone will produce a visually stimulating videotape especially for this purpose. There is such a tape now available for cats, and it actually works pretty well for birds. It has lots of chattering birds and squirrels. My own bird, Portia, a yellow nape, loves the video for cats as well as cartoons, Jeopardy, Family Feud, Tarzan movies, football games, and the William Tell and Thieving Magpie overtures.

If you don't have a timer, leave the radio on all day. It provides some stimulation and is less intrusive than all-day TV. For larger, more intelligent hookbills, however, I believe the television on a timer is better. Paco will not have adequate opportunity for rest if you leave the television on all the time you are gone, but if you set the TV to come on a couple of hours before you get home, the bird will have a little time for independent action, will have used up a little energy, and will be ready to see you, but not demand all your time and all your energy all evening.

That is not to say that you can ignore the bird. Just as a cat that expects attention will "trip" the owner until it receives its expected daily allotment of attention, a bird will communicate its attention needs in unmistakable ways—talking, screaming, banging things around.

To avert the development of problematic screaming, immediately upon returning from work give the bird some one-on-one interaction. Let the bird out of the cage, talk to it, and do a little aerobic exercise. Give the bird a favorite toy that has been withheld during the day and go on about your business, preferably allowing the bird to be in the room with you. If the bird has learned to entertain itself and has not been overnurtured, it will be quite content with side-by-side activities for most of the rest of the evening.

Potty Training

Cookie, an umbrella cockatoo, was always naturally potty trained. Rescued from murderous parents at three days old, he seemed to have an intuitive understanding that he shouldn't relieve himself on people. The now-adult Cookie has never dirtied human clothing with his droppings.

Cookie is unusually perceptive; but potty-trained parrots are becoming less and less uncommon. While cockatoos and macaws are believed to be the easiest, even cockatiels are trainable. As our understanding of parrot behavior increases, so does our ability to modify that behavior. Indeed, many bird people believe that potty training a parrot may be easier than accomplishing the same feat in a male puppy (although owner motivation is not the same).

In the past, potty training birds was in widespread disfavor among caring aviculturists, for although it is easiest to train a parrot to defecate on verbal command, this method is dangerous. Some birds are so eager to please that they will incur life-threatening kidney damage waiting for that verbal command. This becomes an issue if the owner is ill or injured or must go out of town. A forgotten instruction to command the bird to defecate has proved fatal on numerous occasions.

Potty training a companion parrot involves reaching an understanding on the appropriate place to leave that dropping. One may safely train a bird to an approved location (cage or play area) or a visual stimulus—a paper. You must then be sure that the bird has either continuous access to the approved location or paper or that the bird is handled in a manner to accommodate the elimination schedule.

It works like this: each time you want to pick up the bird, place it on its perch or over paper until it eliminates. Some birds do this automatically when first handled. Play with the bird or just keep it with you for about 20 to 30 minutes. Before the bird eliminates again, place it on or over the paper until it goes. Then reward the bird with food or affection.

It helps to know the approximate length of time between droppings. Observation and sensitivity are the keys to this process. You will soon notice changes in the bird's behavior shortly before elimination: the tail will wiggle, the bird will become fidgety. When it is time to defecate, be sure the bird can get to the paper.

It is difficult to remember *not* to say the same thing every time you are waiting for the bird to eliminate. If you repeatedly say something like, "Any time now, dummy," your pet will associate those words with the elimination response, and you will be incorrectly and dangerously training to a verbal command.

Also remember, a parrot can't tell one piece of paper from another, so don't leave important documents lying around. No paper will be safe; but clothes, furniture, and carpeting will be spared a little of the never-ending cleaning.

Recapture: When Your Parrot Flies Away

It is heartrending to watch a beloved feathered companion fly off into the blue. At this moment of high emotion and pumping adrenaline it is most important to remain calm and work quickly.

Try not to lose sight of the bird. A human-dependent parrot will eventually come to someone. If the owner is there, the bird will come to the owner.

Where I live in Colorado, it usually takes at least a few days for a normal companion parrot to figure out where to find food and water. The easiest time to recapture is before the bird learns to forage on its own. Within 48 hours, the bird should be mighty hungry and will come willingly to the owner—*if the owner can get to the bird.*

It is also easier to recapture before the bird, if clipped, regrows additional wing feathers. Sometimes the regrowth of only one primary flight feather on one wing can mean the difference between sailing away and making it only half way across the yard. A new feather can become functional in only a couple of days.

It is helpful to have another like bird, particularly a noisy bird, to try to call the escapee down. A bird extremely bonded to the owner can sometimes be enticed to come down to express jealousy against a known or perceived rival. Larger parrots such as Amazons and macaws will often come to a lure of food or friends and then step up on the offered hand. Set up a food station on a white sheet within the bird's field of vision.

Smaller birds must often be trapped inside a cage with a remote door-closure mechanism. Lure the bird with a like species bird in a small cage inside a larger cage containing food and water.

A larger hookbill will usually fly at dawn and dusk and not much in between. These "flight times" are prime time for recovery. Most birds—particularly larger ones—that are unaccustomed to flying might not quite comprehend flying *down*. Usually, a bird like this is best lured to climb down. Climb as far up to the bird as you can easily. Carefully position yourself so that neither you, the ladder, or the bird will come into contact with power lines.

If you are lucky, you will have to climb down with a possibly angry bird. Wear a solid-colored towel or pillowcase over your shoulders so that it resembles a garment more than a restraint, then take the bird's VFF (very favorite food) up with you.

Try to have on the ground a little family group (containing both loved and hated members of the bird's immediate social group) noisily and delightedly eating foods that the bird likes. Be eating something yourself, crunching and chewing loudly. If the bird is in a tree, tap on the trunk or on a branch so that the bird can feel the vibrations, and lure the bird to you by describing how yummy that food is.

You may have only one chance. Make the most of it. If you once get your hand on the bird, do not let go! You might get a bruise, you might bleed a little, but the odds of having a bone broken are pretty remote and the chance of having a body part "bitten off" is *very* remote. Wrap the bird in the pillowcase or towel as quickly as possible, being sure that the bird is completely contained before beginning the climb down.

If efforts to attract the bird fail, try hosing it down until it is too wet to fly. This sometimes works on poor fliers and birds with large, soft feathers, like cockatoos. A garden hose with a good spray nozzle might work if you can get within 8 or 10 feet (2.4 or 3 m) of the bird. Otherwise don't bother. It will simply leave the poor bird wet in a tree. This is particularly unfortunate in cold weather.

If you must enter someone else's property or borrow equipment such as a ladder, scaffold, or rope, or if you have to hire a cherry picker, you may need a legal all-purpose release of liability. This document should assure all other parties that you and your heirs will not hold anyone responsible for damages of any kind, and that you will be responsible for any damages incurred in the process of recapturing your bird. If someone else is going to climb for you, talk about safety in advance and discuss who would be liable if either the human climber or the bird is accidentally injured.

Always be extremely careful when climbing, whether on your own property or someone else's. Attach a safety rope to tree-climing humans, looped over a sturdy limb and held by volunteers on the ground. Particular care must be taken in the use of metal ladders around power lines, for accidential electrocution is a real danger.

An equipment rental company or a tree service company might be willing to rent equipment to reach the bird. Some fire departments will help; some will not. At least a bird-at-large situation is not yet usually rewarded with a summons and fine.

Pace yourself. Get as much rest and good food as possible. Don't give

up; even if the weather is below freezing, the bird is not going to drop dead just because it spent the night out in the cold. Whether it's a long time or a short time until it is recovered, the bird may come home sick or injured. You may need to be strong for nursing it back to health.

Scooter spent three days at liberty before being rescued by his owner in a cherry picker. He was very hungry and seemed very glad to be home.

Provide Pedialyte or Lactated Ringers or, if it is all you have, Gatorade for the newly recaptured, possibly dehydrated bird. Don't let the bird drink too much too fast. If the bird is weak or was outside wet in cold weather, take it immediately to an avian veterinarian. Some veterinarians are available for emergency counseling during this ordeal and may even provide injectables for you to keep on hand in the event the avian patient is in tough shape when recaptured. This is one more time when a good rapport with that avian veterinarian is very helpful.

If you don't know where the bird is, treat the project as a public relations matter. Make fliers and posters with a good description and photo of the bird. If the bird is rare, it might be best to minimize the value of the bird, perhaps indicating that the bird is mean or in need of regular medication. Try to match the fliers to the people you need to respond to them. If the bird is loose in a poor neighborhood, use handwritten fliers; if the fliers are going to professionals—pet stores, groomers, trainers, veterinarians and bird clubs—try to make them look as professional as possible.

Place advertising in newspapers and local neighborhood and club publications, but don't put the whole leg band number in the ad, as unscrupulous persons might use that information to try to extort the reward money. Advertise a reward and *be prepared* to pay it. Be prepared to pay small rewards to children for spotting the bird. You will probably receive some false leads from children with overactive imaginations, but the children will also be the first to know where the bird is, where it may have been received as stolen goods if it was already recovered, and who has the bird. Even if the children are making up a story, if you slip them a couple of dollars, they will usually be inspired to keep looking for the bird. A surprising number of children will refuse a reward, but try to give them one anyway. Sometimes they will allow you to give their reward money to a parent or sibling because they have been cautioned against taking money from strangers.

Don't give up! Sometimes it takes weeks. The bird will eventually go to someone. If the word has been spread around and the bird is easy to identify positively, it will eventually find its way home. Identification and proof of ownership are very important. Retain the sales slip so that you can prove ownership, and keep a record of the leg band number. If the band fits properly, if it is neither too tight nor too loose, I believe it is best left on the bird for just such emergencies as this.

An identification system involving a computer chip in the bird's chest is now available, but underutilized. I think this form of ID makes lots of sense, particularly for rarer, more difficult to replace birds. Unfortunately, the systems of this type that I have seen require a relatively large, uncomfortable-looking implant. I am not yet convinced that this is safe.

Regular wing feather trims remain the simplest technique for smart bird keepers who prefer that their birds stay safely at home.

Planned Parrothood

News from the American Federation of Aviculture Convention sounds much the same every year: several birds will be added to the endangered species list; we live with less than 30 percent of the species of birds that lived 200 years ago.

There was a time when the newly named endangered birds were those we seldom or never saw in the pet trade—the imperial parrot, Puerto Rican and Cuban Amazons. But every year the names are closer to hearth and home: Moluccan cockatoo, Patagonian conure, Mexican redhead; there are persistent rumors about the Goffin's cockatoo.

In addition to loss of habitat, there are rumors of overtrapping for the pet trade. Pending legislation could ban all imports for the pet trade into the United States. The intent of this legislation is honorable but, I believe, misdirected. It is my understanding and belief that the greatest threat to wild birds is habitat destruction, and usually that means agriculture. Even a bird that is abundant today may be a victim of "agricultural progress" tomorrow. Many birds considered pest species will be killed in their native range if we destroy their monetary value. Like our own Carolina parakeet, which became extinct as a result of "agricultural progress" in the United States by 1917, they may be eradicated for the protection of farms and ranches.

But agriculture isn't the only way birds lose habitat. Only a dozen years ago the Mexican redhead, or green-cheeked Amazon, was inexpensive and apparently abundant. In the 1970s it was a frequent traveler

through the pet trade in most of the United States. In the early 1980s the Mexican government banned exportation of native species, greatly reducing the number of legal green-cheeks to reach the pet trade. But even with official government motivation to protect birds, it is increasingly difficult to preserve the habitat that ensures their survival. Today, the green-cheek's breeding grounds are being developed for residential use. Because of the dwindling size of the Mexican redhead's habitat, it is not inconceivable that one large-scale ecological disaster, such as a chemical spill or tropical storm, could effectively eradicate this species in the wild.

It is therefore reasonable to advise the owner of an exotic species suffering from loss of habitat to make an effort to facilitate the bird's reproduction. The Mexican redhead, like many exotic birds, is well-suited to life indoors. Most individuals are adorable little clowns, although hormones may render them seasonally unpredictable, usually in their teens. They breed readily in captivity, and should have a good chance for long-term survival—depending on their human companions' ability and willingness to provide for their reproductive needs.

First, since most parrots have no external sexual characteristics, gender must be determined through surgery or other scientific sexing technique. Then a compatible, same-species mate must be obtained. Dispositional changes, courtship, and mo-

nogamous, lifetime pairing in these long-lived creatures consume much time, space, and energy. Some owners of truculent teenage parrots acquire mates for these treasured avian companions and set them up in housekeeping in the living room or basement. Some allow their pet to go to the "in-laws" (owners of the bird's mate), expecting a hand-fed baby in return for their sacrifice.

Maybe these birds, so well-suited to captivity, are in their last natural habitat—our shared living spaces. Or maybe in a few years we will be training our captive-bred baby birds to reclaim the forests. Not all our "Lonely Hearts Club" parrots will have the desire or ability for reproduction, but it is our responsibility to allow them to try.

Chapter 8

Stories

The Day Kitty Flew Away

Miss Kitty is a Gray-cheeked parakeet, a tiny Andean parrot with an uneven disposition and raucous voice.

Although she had been "in the family" for a number of years, I had inherited her only a week before. Assuming responsibility for such a creature with so many emotional strings attached is a frightening experience, particularly if she decides to fly away.

What kind of person would allow a cat or dog out without supervision or would not clip a pet bird's wing feathers?

A foolish and neglectful one.

Such a careless bird keeper sometimes experiences the horror of watching a pet bird sneak through an open doorway and sail out into the blue.

I felt pretty silly running through the neighborhood searching the skies calling, "Here, Kitty, Kitty." (But I was *very glad* her previous owners had changed her name which was formerly "Sweet Baby Jesus.")

A "kitty" with a voice like a loud, squeaky metal hinge is pretty easy to track. Within minutes I could hear, but not see her. Trespassing in a neighbor's yard, I nearly stepped on her, then watched as she flew around the house and out of sight.

But again, that voice gave her position away. Soon I could make out a little blue head on a windy bough 3 or 4 feet (about 1 m) above a power line. The power line bordered an enclosure containing a rottweiler, a German shepherd, and a basset hound, all vigorously protesting whenever I stepped too near their yard.

It was a very windy day, and to top it all off, my voice was giving out. Sitting on a driveway adjacent to the site of this multi-pet fiasco, I realized that it might take a while to coax Miss Kitty down. I returned home for Polly (my second noisiest unbonded bird), Kitty's cage, a handful of grapes, some ice cream, Coca-Cola, and my electronic pager—all of Kitty's favorite things.

I spent the afternoon eating and talking to a chattering lory (Crackers) in a stranger's driveway and repeatedly paging a small parrot in a tall tree.

I thought she was about to come down when she started saying "Com'ere" back and forth to the pager. And once, in desperation, I tried to climb the tree; but when I jumped down, Kitty must have flown, for suddenly she had disappeared.

Terrified and dejected, I started home with all my stuff.

But again I heard that screechy, metallic voice from a bush a few houses over on the other side of the block.

Miss Kitty had gone to a multi-generational lawn party complete with a swarm of elementary-school-age children. They were clustered around a bush, pointing, exclaiming, and throwing small objects.

By the time I ran around the block, adults also were hurrying to one side of the house. As I approached the high wire fence, I saw Miss Kitty sitting in one of the chain links, a look of terror in her eyes as she watched three children, just slightly too short, reaching for her.

With a squawk of relief and recognition, Kitty stepped up on my hand and did what she likes to do best.

Bite me.

Portia Got the Part

The Denver Chamber Orchestra and Opera Colorado were to perform "Amahl and the Night Visitors," a story set in the Holy Land and relating to the birth of Jesus. The script called for a parrot in a cage. Could I supply one?

The answer was a qualified "Yes." My favorite, Portia, was available, but being a New World bird, her species could not have attended the birth of Jesus in the Middle East. Muffin, my cockatiel, was also an impossible candidate for similar historical and geographical reasons. My only Old World parrot, Tom Foolery, a lovebird, was too small to be seen on stage.

It was time to acquire that African ringneck I had wanted for so long. A local pet store had ringnecks in stock; armed with my checkbook I was there within the hour. The remaining bird was rather disappointing—in poor feather, with no trace of a ring around its neck. I decided to look further and called a friendly wholesaler who, I hoped, could refer me to a retail store with ringnecks.

"I don't know anyone," he said, "but I have a pair, and the one I thought was a female just developed color. I'm looking for someone with a female to trade for a male."

It was time to talk turkey. I bought the colorless specimen and traded her to the wholesaler for his lovely rose-ringed male in perfect feather.

An old British parrot book confirmed that ringnecks were highly prized during the time of the Roman Empire and that they were kept in "ornate cages." I was convinced that I had found the perfect bird for the opera *and* the perfect cage. The evening of dress rehearsal I delivered the African ringneck in a tall, square wrought iron cage with a domed top. It was lovely, but it weighed about 25 pounds.

I didn't know that the page who was

to carry the bird also had to carry a lantern, a staff, a sack, and a carpet. I also didn't know that he had to carry them through the audience from the back of a large two-story hall. The ringneck wound up in a small budgie cage.

Adding insult to injury, the director complained that the bird was too small and was not really what they had in mind. The bird the producer described—the bird the producer wanted—was an Amazon.

Authenticity was the loser; I was asked to provide a parrot from a part of the world unknown until about 1500 years after the time of the opera!

I explained that Portia loved singing, and that he might break into any one of several "rolls" during the performance. He has a large vocabulary, including such favorites as "Oh, what a pretty bird!" (running 5 to 15 minutes); the "Clean up your cage/Shut-up!" interchange (audible for several floors of my apartment building); and "Somewhere Over the Rainbow" in off-key falsetto.

The risk of being upstaged by a parrot was a small price to pay for such a fine bird. Portia was the bird the producer wanted; Portia was the one he got.

The parrot in "Amahl" and its slightly hard-of-hearing owner provided comic relief in the inspirational story. Portia had only two responsibilities—to take food (a role my slightly obese parrot was born for) and to be quiet. I wasn't so sure about the quiet part.

The opulent production took place on two cold December nights in the beautiful Trinity Church, a national historic landmark. The sanctuary is a masterpiece of turn-of-the-century woodwork and stained glass. Enormous brass organ pipes formed a gleaming backdrop for the stage, the esteemed maestra JoAnn Falleta, and her orchestra.

Waiting in darkness backstage, Portia was nearly perfect. A few times he inquired quietly, "What?" but he spoke so softly that only I could hear him.

On stage, too, Portia was perfect the first night, accepting food and eating it quietly. But that was just the first night.

The second performance was not sold out, and I managed a seat in the audience with a friend. As the royal procession entered, I knew to expect trouble. As the page wobbled his way to the stage, we could see that the cage was not completely covered! I braced myself for the worst.

My friend kept saying "What did Portia say?" and "I'm sure he said something." But alas, I did not hear him. My untrained ear had missed Portia's faux pas.

No, Portia didn't break into "Somewhere Over the Rainbow"; he didn't scream "Shut Up!" at the tenor. But members of the orchestra reported that when each of the kings knocked on Amahl's door that cold Christmas night, a sweet, clear parrot's voice called out—on all three occasions—"Come in."

Redheads, Blondes, and "The Thunderbolt"

Parrots have some striking idiosyncrasies that seem more human than traits documented in other companion animals. For one thing, parrots put a lot of stock in hair color. It is not uncommon to encounter a parrot who will either attack redheads or court them. The same is true to a lesser extent of blondes; I have found that Amazons in particular seem inordinately attracted to blondes.

The attraction to hair color, however, is not nearly so curious as the parrot's predisposition to fall immediately, completely, head-over-heels in love at first sight. This phenomenon is called "The Thunderbolt." I have seen it in intelligent, well-socialized, bonded parrots such as my own yellow nape. It has also been documented in African grays, macaws, most common companion Amazons, cockatoos, and even lovebirds, cockatiels, and budgies.

This is the way it happened with Portia.

Once, during a move to a new home that was not yet ready, Portia (my life companion yellow nape), Moan Eek (my hand-fed Dutch blue lovebird), and I stayed briefly with our friend June in her downtown duplex. It was summer, and I was sunbathing on the front lawn with a book, a cool drink, and my cordless phone. Portia, not comprehending that there was no shade outside, was letting me know in no uncertain terms that he was not pleased to be left inside. The front door was open, and Portia was screaming at top volume including few words except an occasional "Shut up"—which sometimes sounded a little like "Help."

Suddenly, inexplicably, Portia was quiet. I heard the front door bang hard against the wall. Rushing into the living room I found a striking, athletic blonde woman with dark-rimmed glasses standing beside Portia's cage holding a baseball bat in a very threatening posture.

"I thought someone was being attacked," she said with an expression somehow combining relief and disbelief; "I thought June needed help!"

I explained that the birds and I were staying with June for a few days and apologized for disturbing her day.

Portia was immediately smitten —begging, twirling, pinpointing, fanning his tail, spreading his wings in full display.

June's neighbor was an accountant who worked at home. She introduced herself and went back to work. Portia and I went on about our business and forgot the incident—or so I thought.

A few weeks later, on the Fourth of July, June decided to give a party, and the neighbor was invited. Portia and I arrived early to help with food. Portia took his position on a very high curtain rod in the nonsmoking room. By the time the blonde neighbor arrived, the room was crowded, but Portia instantly acknowledged her entry with a loud scream. Of course, the neighbor had to tell the story of the beautiful parrot who was nearly attacked—or maybe rescued from boredom—with a baseball bat.

I took the opportunity to encourage Portia to entertain the crowd with his rendition of "Somewhere Over the Rainbow." As he pinpointed, displayed, and postured in the direction of the beautiful woman with whom he was smitten, I said, "Portia, sing for us."

Instead of launching directly into his usual off-key falsetto, Portia, eyes flashing like a Las Vegas casino sign said, "Portia, sing for us!" Then he sang "Somewhere Over the Rainbow."

Portia and I had a marvelous relationship, and he was devoted to me; but I know if he had had a choice at that party, he would have gone home with June's blonde neighbor.

From that moment on, those words became a permanent part of Portia's riff. He is mated now, but if the moment is right and the mood strikes him, he still says, "Portia, sing for us" before he sings "Somewhere Over the Rainbow."

I sometimes fancy that Portia thinks of his "lady love lost" when he repeats those words today. More likely, he is merely singing a "song" he learned when he was trying to impress June's beautiful blonde neighbor by repeating those words he had learned to say *the first time he ever heard them*.

The Gray Parrot Who Wouldn't Talk

Zorba is a 12-year-old African gray parrot, a species known for its exceptional ability to acquire human speech. The first time I saw him, on April 7, 1992, he didn't talk.

A full-flighted creature who lived at liberty in a spacious, high-ceilinged home, Zorba was apparently emotionally well-adjusted. He was neither nippy, noisy, nor aggressive. Zorba's failure to talk didn't seem to stem from depression. He had simply made his own way and was not motivated to communicate with people. During the ten years he had lived with Dave and Susan, he had trained people to leave him alone by growling at any approach.

The previous Christmas, Zorba's family had been reduced by circumstance from two humans and four companion animals to two humans and two animals. Treasuring the balance and quality of their home environment, the humans embarked, not on a program to find new animals, but on a "pet conservation" program to improve the survivability and quality of life of the remaining animals. Zorba and Ilsa, the 11-year-old German shepherd, benefited from increased attention and companionship.

With a disposition more like a basset hound than a shepherd, Ilsa was just about the sweetest dog I had ever seen. It was always clear that she had a special relationship with Zorba.

We didn't know at the time that Zorba's love for Ilsa would signal the opening of a door to communication with humans.

Zorba controlled a sunny entry hall by growling at anyone who came too close, a situation that left concerned humans forever rushing through the noisy, bird-controlled space. While he didn't live in his cage, he did choose to spend all his time on top of it. Although some avian writers suggest that confining a parrot to a cage can stimulate the bird to talk, we didn't want to risk depression. I couldn't see locking Zorba up to teach him to talk.

Starting that April evening, Zorba's owners, Susan and Dave, decided to make environmental changes designed to stimulate the adolescent nontalking parrot to communicate with them. Zorba was induced to establish larger territory—including emotional territory—in the home by showering, eating, and sleeping in the same room with Susan, Dave, and Ilsa. At home wherever they went, the bird went too.

We did not change everything immediately. Although most avian consultants recommended trimming wing feathers, in this case I felt that Zorba might be more easily motivated if few restrictions were placed on him. It is an uncommon tack in the treating of parrot behavior problems (which usually include aggression). The bird was also shown video tapes of African gray parrots mimicking and speaking English words. Susan and Dave also chose to help Zorba attend "flock (group) therapy" for gray parrots—driving 120 miles once a month—to accommodate their "autistic" adolescent.

When he first saw another of his kind—for the first time in 11 years—Zorba flew across the room to visit Roger, a "toddler" gray parrot being treated for demanding all his human "mom's" attention. In typical "terrible twos" fashion, Roger attacked Zorba, and spent most of their first meeting demonstrating that he was boss on the table and basket perches.

It was a different story, however, when they did the "find-mom-in-the-hallways" exercise. Zorba preened and strutted like a teenage dandy while Roger pitty-patted around like a little lost wind-up toy.

During the second month Susan and Dave reported that Zorba practiced many, many new sounds. The diversity and duration of the sounds seemed in some ways to relate to Ilsa's coming and going in the mornings. Zorba's interest in other animals was easily observed in the hall exercises.

We decided to try to induce Roger, the parrot, to teach Zorba to talk in group. Situating Roger just out of sight of all birds and people, the loquacious toddler performed as expected, entertaining the group with Rogerisms like "Hi, Rog," "Bonjou....," "What," and "Hel-lo-o" (in Amazonian).

During the following month, an unhappy little bit of "life" came along that obviously influenced Zorba's talking therapy. Ilsa disappeared. The elderly dog was terrified of thunder and became lost from her yard during a noisy summer storm. Dave and Susan plastered the area with fliers and talked to everyone in a five-mile radius of their rural mountain home. Extensive, exhausting, and unsuccessful searches were made daily.

Zorba was devastated. There was no more morning "talking practice." Sometimes when Susan and Dave were out of the room, they thought they could hear a baby cry. They were soon able to verify that their 12-year-old bird's only sounds during that time were the sounds of a human infant crying. It was a sound that the bird had never heard in their home.

Only a few days before gray parrot group therapy in July, an emotionally disturbed Ilsa found her way home. Her collar, which was upside down, had obviously been removed and replaced. Zorba was much cheered, spending the next few days talking and bumping beaks with a floor-level mirror he had never noticed before.

The evening of group therapy, Susan and Dave were torn between nursing their obviously upset shepherd and making the four-hour round trip to parrot group. Leaving Ilsa with friends, they arrived on time, situating Zorba's basket at the head of the big oak table in the conference room. Well after the start of the meeting,

Roger and his owner entered the room, placing Roger on a lower basket next to Zorba.

Zorba took one look, leaned over and said—in his best belly-up to the bar, good-ole-boy voice—"Hi, Rog!" The room erupted in laughter, applause, and tears.

Zorba's first two human words were used with cognition on July 15, 1992. During the next month Zorba was given his own "bird mirror," a shiny slab of metal on a chain, as companionship in his cage. By the next morning after the addition of his new companion in the mirror, he was saying both "Hello" and "Corn."

Zorba and Roger in "flock therapy."

Useful Literature and Addresses

Books

Gallerstein, Gary A.: *Bird Owners Home and Health Care*, Howell Book House Inc., New York, 1986.

Low, Rosemary: *The Complete Book of Parrots*, Barron's, Hauppauge, 1989.

Vriends, Matthew M., PhD: *Popular Parrots*, Howell Book House Inc., New York, 1989.

————: *The New Cockatiel Handbook*, Barron's, Hauppauge, 1989.

Wolter Annette: *Parrots*, Barron's, Hauppauge, 1992.

Magazines

American Cage Bird Magazine
One Glamore Court
Smithtown, NY 11787

The AFA Watchbird
2208 "A" Artesia Blvd.
Redondo Beach, CA 90278

Bird Talk
P.O. Box 6050
Mission Viejo, CA 92690

Pet Bird Report
2236 Mariner Square Drive #35
Alameda, CA 94501

Positively Pets
1201 East Colfax
Denver, CO 80218

Organizations

American Cockatiel Society, Inc.
The Editor
1801 19th Ave. N.E.
Minneapolis, MN 55418

American Federation of Aviculture
P.O. Box 1568
Redondo Beach, CA 90278

Association of Avian Veterinarians
P.O. Box 811720
Boca Raton, FL 33481

National Cockatiel Society
Rt. 1 Box 412
Equality, AL 36026

National Parrot Association
8 North Hoffman Lane
Hauppauge, NY 11788

Index

Page references in **boldface** indicate color photos.